Revoice: L the Involute Carrier of Reality

Kernfisk Oehnrloera

MAPLE
PUBLISHERS

Revoice: Uncurling The Involute Carrier of Reality

Author: Kernfisk Oehnrloera

Copyright © Kernfisk Oehnrloera (2024)

The right of Kernfisk Oehnrloera to be identified as author of this work has been asserted by the author in accordance with section 77 and 78 of the Copyright, Designs and Patents Act 1988.

First Published in 2024

ISBN 978-1-83538-087-1 (Paperback)
      978-1-83538-088-8 (E-Book)

Book Layout by:
> White Magic Studios
> www.whitemagicstudios.co.uk

Published by:
> Maple Publishers
> Fairbourne Drive, Atterbury,
> Milton Keynes,
> MK10 9RG, UK
> www.maplepublishers.com

A CIP catalogue record for this title is available from the British Library.

All rights reserved. No part of this book may be reproduced or translated by any form or by any means, electronic or mechanical, including photocopying, recording or by any information storage and retrieval system without written permission from the author.

The views expressed in this work are solely those of the author and do not reflect the opinions of Publishers, and the Publisher hereby disclaims any responsibility for them.

For seekers of mental yoke-melting and uncanniness:

Perception is brain-projected simulations of reality, and voices are in need of flexibility and trained, non-hijacked freedom of choices to take and shift shapes, which should contribute to the equilibrating of whichever surrounding mechanisms by design. Fiction, or non-fiction; how about starting with non-identifying and coexisting with all range of voice variants so as to approximate to the essence of reality, before touching the untouchable realness and unrealness and the many emotions bound to them?

GEOGRAPHICAL DISTRIBUTION OF

North America

North Atlantic Ocean

Atlantis

Pacific Ocean

South America

South Atlantic Ocean

Two Global System Clusters

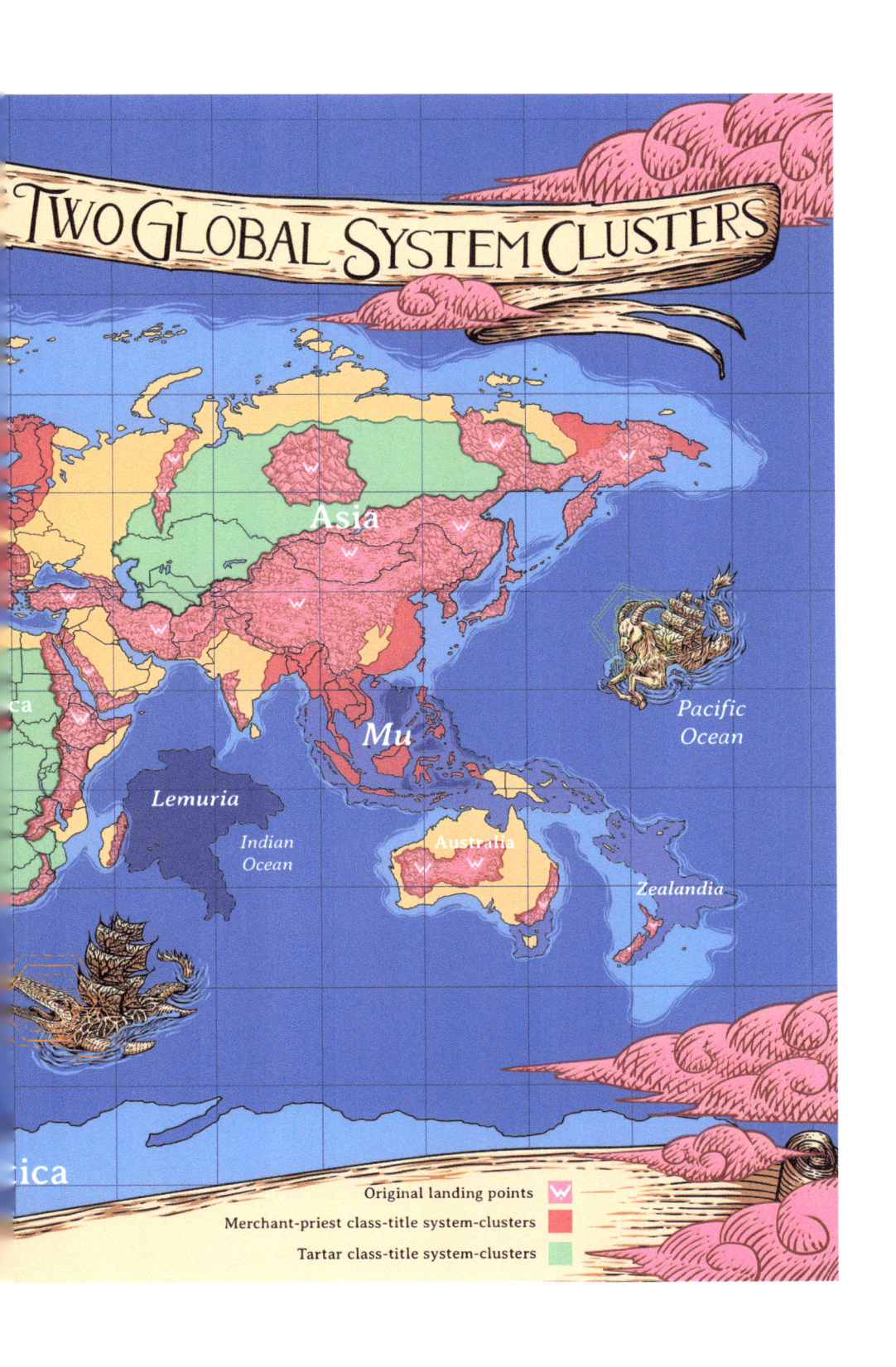

Asia

Mu

Pacific Ocean

Lemuria

Indian Ocean

Australia

Zealandia

Original landing points
Merchant-priest class-title system-clusters
Tartar class-title system-clusters

Table of Contents

Card Kerrep Lerats I

Penetrating Linear Perceptions: Reconstructing the Brain-like Folds of What Happened in our Past — 11 – 62

Card Kerrep Sewl I-1 — 11
Are all the system and sub-systems really that fixed?

Card Kerrep Sewl I-2 — 11
Where actually are the Tartar civilisation-systems?

Card Kerrep Sewl I-3 — 12
Where actually are the Survival Civilisation civilisation-systems?

Card Kerrep Sewl I-4 — 13
What prompted the Survival Civilisation to be surviving?

Card Kerrep Sewl I-5 — 13
What are civilisation class-title systems?

Card Kerrep Sewl I-6 — 14
How different from or similar to the contemporary civilisation systems were the ancient civilisation class-title systems?

Card Kerrep Sewl I-7 — 16
Why have the Jews and Hakkas been global presences?

Card Kerrep Sewl I-8 — 23
Why are similar linguistic features of language spread out on the globe?

Card Kerrep Sewl I-9 — 26
Why was the one-piece robe a shared costume feature among the many class-title system clusters under merchant-priest and Tartar?

Card Kerrep Sewl I-10 — 28
Why were mythological features shared among different branches of the merchant-priest class-title system-clusters?

Card Kerrep Sewl I-11 30
Why are floods a shared theme among world mythologies?

Card Kerrep Sewl I-12 32
Why did cultural-layer rich Himalayan Central Branch Restoration civilisations play minor roles in the world historically?

Card Kerrep Sewl I-13 40
Why were the Gosford Glyphs discovered in Australia?

Card Kerrep Sewl I-14 41
What are the connections between the Egyptian Theban legion and the Moors? Why is the supposedly East Asian black-and-white, Kuahroom-Laong-styled symbol in the Book of Changes found on Theban legion flouting?

Card Kerrep Sewl I-15 42
What could Athanasius Kircher's theory of the Egyptian hieroglyphs-oracle-bones-script imply?

Card Kerrep Sewl I-16 42
Why do the Tamil-speaking Dravidians physically look like the Australian aborigines?

Card Kerrep Sewl I-17 43
Why was there the lack of writing system in Northern Europe before the invention of Runic script?

Card Kerrep Sewl I-18 44
Why is Finland considered the location of Troy and Sweden and the Baltic shores Greek-Achaeans?

Card Kerrep Sewl I-19 46
Why were there so many cultural similarities between the Carthage-based Phoenicians and the Venice-based Venetian merchants?

Card Kerrep Sewl I-20 47
What was the role of Morocco and Egypt in the merchant-priest class-title system-clusters?

Card Kerrep Sewl I-21   49
Why were there two versions of the portrait of Napoleon, one fair-skinned and one dark-skinned?

Card Kerrep Sewl I-22   50
What did the Dutch discovery of Australia, Tasmania and New Zealand symbolise?

Card Kerrep Sewl I-23   52
What fuelled the Anglo-Dutch war other than rivalry and trade wars?

Card Kerrep Sewl I-24   53
Why did Nazi Germany take interest in Antarctica (beginning with Neuschwabenland) and Himalayan Bhö as it rose to a sea power that could challenge the British?

Card Kerrep Sewl I-25   54
What preserved the remnants of Tartar system-clusters and vitalised them?

Card Kerrep Sewl I-26   55
What is the contemporary shadow Tartar state aside from the one in mainland East Asia?

Card Kerrep Lerats II Erosion-reversing: Dialling into the Lost Faces of Mythologies and Religions   62 – 73

Card Kerrep Sewl II-1   62
What lies beyond the lava-filled crust and cores of the Earth?

Card Kerrep Sewl II-2   63
Why have there been records of encounters with higher dimensions?

Card Kerrep Sewl II-3   66
How does the extra-terrestrial entity relate to those within planet Earth?

Card Kerrep Sewl II-4   68
Why was cynocephaly a widespread phenomenon throughout world mythologies and folklore?

Card Kerrep Sewl II-5   70

What is dimensional-shifting and its connection with the 'Absolute'?

Card Kerrep Sewl II-6   72

How do the many layers of Hindu mythological hell relate to accessing Agartha?

Card Kerrep Lerats III Unsolved mysteries: Midland between Coincidences and the Pre-determined   74 – 78

Card Kerrep Sewl III-1   74

Why are certain geographical locations prone to choices of spiritual practise and supernatural sightings?

Card Kerrep Sewl III-2   75

What role do the flying head entities play in Earth's trial system?

Card Kerrep Sewl III-3   76

What lies beyond the symbolic stories in Finnish mythology and East Asian folklore?

Card Kerrep Lerats V The Bloated Detachment of the Supernatural from Us: Codes within Us that Link to the Ground of Reality   78 – 83

Card Kerrep Sewl V-1   78

What is the structure of reality made of?

Card Kerrep Sewl V-2   81

Why have locations with enclosed natures been chosen for long-term meditation throughout history?

Card Kerrep Sewl V-3   82

What are the mental effects of changes in physical human body structure?

Card Kerrep Lerats IV Fears towards the Shattering of our Body Structure: What Is the Truth behind Diseases?   83 – 88

Card Kerrep Sewl IV-1   83

How are Homo sapiens connected with Homo Subterraneous?

Card Kerrep Sewl IV-2 85
What are the perceived causes of Wooden Disease?

Card Kerrep Sewl IV-3 87
Why were there records of 'moving wooden artefacts' throughout history?

Card Kerrep Lerats II Erosion-reversing: Dialling into the Lost Faces of Mythologies and Religions 88 – 94

Card Kerrep Sewl II-7 89
How is unlocking DNA and consciousness related to the construction of ancient mega structures?

Card Kerrep Sewl II-8 91
Who were the guardians against the distortion / corruption of the original last-cycle civilisation religions?

Card Kerrep Sewl II-9 93
Who were the dark sages during the times of distortion / corruption of the original last-cycle civilisation religions?

Card Kerrep Lerats III Unsolved mysteries: Midland between Coincidences and the Pre-determined 94 – 97

Card Kerrep Sewl III-4 94
Why were records of spirit possessions from animals widespread among world mythologies and folklores?

Card Kerrep Sewl III-5 96
What are the roles of the sentient animals?

Card Kerrep Lerats I

Penetrating Linear Perceptions: Reconstructing the Brain-like Folds of What Happened in our Past

Card Kerrep Sewl I-1

Are all the system and sub-systems really that fixed?

The shared systemic concept of McDonald's-corporatism and Tartar-non-Tartar class-title system clusters

Tartaria and its Coastal Insular Merchant-Priest Class-title Rival: Building upon the Destabilised Last-cycle Civilisation

Although it is something that we have not been conditioned to do, chronologic based history should, I believe, be read or interpreted symbolically instead of taken literally. This will get us closer to what actually happened. This premise is highlighted in the title of the book from Anatoly T. Fomenko: History, Fiction, or Science?

Card Kerrep Sewl I-2

Where actually are the Tartar civilisation-systems?

Geographical Range of Tartaria (Continental Eurasia-Americas)

This is an area that stretches across Siberia, inland North America excluding its western coastal region, from Alaska to as far south as Oregon and later Himalayan Bhö and its eastern periphery – the inland portion of East Asia, south of southern Mongolia, the Teew People; Teew as in /*tiw/ according to Baxter–Sagart's reconstruction. All names related to this civilisation would be in the reconstructed version, to resonate with its non-Tartar past, as opposed to a shadow Tartar, now.

Card Kerrep Sewl I-3
Where actually are the Survival Civilisation civilisation-systems?

Geographical Range of the Survival Civilisation (Coastal and Insular Eurasia-Americas)

Let's start to visualise long-stretching brushes on the map from the coastal area of Southeast Asia, stretching from Indonesia, the Philippines and coastal Vietnam in the south, to coastal mainland East Asian Staon-Rooes-Teroong Liryou-Woaat people to the north.

A breakdown of the complex ancient East Asian territorial clusters are as follow: Staon, or Shang Dynasty, was a semi-tribal state, Staon as in /*s-taŋ/ according to Baxter–Sagart reconstruction; Teroong Liryou (Dongyi), a semi-tribal state living in juxtaposition with the Staon, Liryou as in /*ləj/ according to Baxter–Sagart reconstruction; Rooes (later State of Lai), a semi-tribal state belonging to the Teroong Liryou who lived in juxtaposition with the Staon, Rooes as in /*ruːs/ according to Baxter–Sagart reconstruction; Woaat the Yue people (genetically Kra–Dai), Woaat as in /*[ɢ]ʷat/ according to Baxter–Sagart reconstruction. Rooes among the system clusters stands out in its transitory geographic, genetic and cultural states where Jomon-Japonic, Kra–Dai and Austronesian groups coexisted along side one another; this was also the name of a place within the belt that would later appear as Dzaeriryou (the Ch'I ancient mainland East Asian civilisation later) across from the Korean peninsula (Jomon-Japonic before being displaced by the Koreanic People who were themselves fleeing from the eastward-pushing Saka-Teew-Tartars).

All the above-mentioned geographical locations form a horse-shoe shape region, a part of a bigger belt that would be completed by the Japanese archipelago (Jomon-Ainu), Sakhalin Island, Kamchatka peninsula, Arctic coast of western Siberia (Samoyedic people and Sami People), coastal Alaska (Taku, meaning Geese Flood Upriver Tribe), coastal Pacific north west (Tlingit), and Olmec; all belonging to the priest-wizard-merchant global class that inherited and stubbornly survived as they moved to periphery, or more remote place away from the original heartlands of the last-cycle civilisation post great flood.

Card Kerrep Sewl I-4
What prompted the Survival Civilisation to be surviving?

Common Topographic Features of the Geographical Distribution of the Restoration Survival Civilisations

After the great flood, recorded in mythology, religion and written and spoken folklore around the world, the people who survived looked for plateaus and mountains, or areas near the poles, in particular in Greenland. They moved to areas that they saw as either elevated from the flood water, or frozen and chose these places to relocate to.

Card Kerrep Sewl I-5
What are civilisation class-title systems?

Looking at the Concept of Rivalling Class-Title and Systems

The dynamic of the rivalry between different global class-title system clusters could have been the heritage of the time before the global last-cycle civilisation started to decline, where different versions of class-title system clusters existed.

It could even have been different tiers from one system spinning off to establish a new system through internal sub-division competing for prestige, as part of a manifestation of cultural openness and flexibility, under that global last-cycle civilisation.

Card Kerrep Sewl I-6

How different from or similar to the contemporary civilisation systems were the ancient civilisation class-title systems?

How do the Tartar class-title system and the rivalling priest-merchant class-title system, function?

What cultural traits do they possess?

What has to be perceived when convergent evolution is looked through as one of many, instead of the sole cause of the shared cultural traits?

Tartar – a Global Warrior-nomadic Class-title System and their Many Successors, Found Notably on the Eurasian Steppes, with the Inland Americas being its Periphery

Imagine the many managers of McDonald's branches globally, establishing their own versions of the brand (not a logo, but countless versions in the minds of the customers) operating in the same fast-food industry landscape.

Now think of a Tartar. Historically, the term Tatar was given to anyone who originated from the vast Northern and Central Asian landmass which at that time was known as Tartary, a term also connected to the Mongol Empire itself. The Tartars invented the nomadic lifestyle as well as horseback warfare.

The Scythians are also well known in history – or in myth. Flourishing from about 900 to 200BC, they ranged from their homelands in Siberia to the Black Sea and mainland East Asia. The nomadic lifestyle of their earlier predecessors proto-systems, the Yamnaya Culture (3300 – 2600 BC) and especially Srubnaya culture (1900 – 1200 BC) was where the use of chariots started to emerge. This could be seen as the intense nomadic system slowly forming while being experimental in its gradual rise to prominence. This nomadic people's claim to fame is that they pioneered more sophisticated saddles that were preserved for the elite warriors as a symbol of their achievements in battles, because they could manoeuvre without saddles, as with other warriors who had a very high skills in fighting. This allowed them to fight better, on horseback, than any settled civilisations, the merchant-priest class-title system-clusters they came up against.

They came before the ancestral predecessor of the Hun, the Kuahong Nera (or Huna, the ancestral class-title of the later Huns), Noonan, Rouran, in the reconstructed language (proto-Mongolic-Tungusic) and the proto-Turkic and Tungusic including the Seewkdeens, a reconstructed rendering of the Shushen People, ancestral to the later Jurchen-Manchus, who created their own sub-system.

One such nomadic-Tartar class-title group, the ancestors of the Teroong Gehera and Seewkdeens groups, a reconstructed rendering of the Donghu People and Sushen (Proto-Tungusic-Mongolic group located in present day southern Manchuria), were pulled into the priest-merchant-class sphere of influence as they practised oracle bone divination (this involved preparing oracle bones, first drilling and then polishing the bones before heating them), or scapulimancy, a feature found in priest-merchant-class title throughout the survival civilisations, notably in Staon class-title system clusters in coastal mainland East Asia, right across the Korean peninsula. Scapulimancy involves telling a fortune from the scapula bone. This tradition has roots in ancient civilisations in mainland East Asia where broader class-title identity there was itself forming, or a Proto-Blossom-People State as they call themselves, together with North America and Central Asia. Ethnographic research and historical chronicles studied, on scapulimancy in Central Asia, has archaeologists assigning a ritual meaning to scapulae found in which regular perforations are present.

Scapulimancy is also found in the North American Mistassini Cree people, located in the sub-Arctic Canadian coastal regions surrounding the Hudson Bay and stretching to the coast of Labrador, in a priest-merchant class-title group who were the North American Tartars' rival. They employed the use of bone reading to foresee events in the future in the same way as was seen with the Staon group in coastal mainland East Asia, with their neighbouring Naskapi Innu people also performing this practise but without prophesising.

Early North American inland indigenous groups who were in the nomadic-Tartar class-title system clusters could also have been horse-riding until the coastal merchant-priest-class cut them off from their Eurasian Tartar cousin groups, ending the supply of horses and the skill to breed them.

This possibly turned them into solely bison-riding groups causing the priest-merchant class-title groups to label them 'bison-hunters' to make them look barbaric and so that they could monopolise bison-riding themselves as a means of preserving the knowledge they inherited from last-cycle civilisations.

The non-Tartar North American indigenous class-title groups had a better chance of semi-domesticating the bison, creating a relationship similar to that between humans and cats, with the know-how inherited from the last-cycle civilisations fading only gradually.

The emergence of the Tartar class-title system clusters could be seen as post-great flood development of the peripheral, more backward regions, contemporary to when last-cycle civilisations were still prosperous. This had been achieved through domestication of horses and the consequential invention of the nomadic-lifestyle, both built upon what they inherited from the last-cycle civilisation refugees that had fled there following the epoch of the rising sea level.

One can identify costume, rituals, art styles and linguistic similarities between the coastal dwelling groups and those that lived inland as well as a much stronger awareness to preserve the last-cycle civilisation when compared to the Tartaria regions of the restoration centres civilisation, the priest-merchant class-title system clusters. There were also linguistic similarities between the names of the class-titles groups and their variants' assimilation into either the survival civilisation restoration centres, or Tartaria (the pull-and-push effect). One can, of course, say that these are the results of convergent evolution. This, however, would be too broad an umbrella term and too much of a flat, linear concept, if it was the only thinking process on which simulation of what actually happened in the past was based.

Card Kerrep Sewl I-7

Why have the Jews and Hakkas been global presences?

Why are there inexplicable linguistic similarities between the different names of the class-title system-clusters scattered globally?

Why didn't their cultural traits divert from one another due to the geographical stretch?

The afore-mentioned class-title system-clusters concepts could apply to Saka / Hakka, Stein-Jew / Aleutian / Staon-Dzaeriryou and Teew.

Such class-title system clusters would often have multiple, similar variants of names found occurring in different corners of the world where similar norms, beliefs, rituals, and costumes were seen.

Different class-title sub-systems, describing similar castes, for example, the merchant-priest class union could be a result of flexibility in different sub-class-titles, or sub-class-title systems as they cooperated and competed. This is further complicated by the push-and-pull relationship that existed between the survival civilisation and the newly emerging Tartaria, both of which adopted variations of the global class-title system clusters in their own civilisation system. Similar phonetic features can be found scattered around the world such as:

- 'Aleu' from the Aleutian',
- 'Zaeriryou from the successor of the Staon, Dzaeriryou',
- 'Teew', 'Jew', 'Judah';
- 'Staon' and the later 'Stein'

These are all linguistic depictions allocated to the prominent earliest merchant-priest class-title system clusters, before the eventual degeneration that occurred over the generations either because of harsh geography, a loss of grasp on last-cycle civilisation cultures, or influence by and partial absorption into Tartaria (the Tartar class-title system clusters).

By the time they'd spread to the western sections of the Loess Plateau, the Teew were an interesting case. Their ancestor's name was Pir Alood, the reconstructed rendering of Buzhu. There was a similarity between its class-title name and the Pir Teew Mountain, also known as the Unrevolving Mountain, where the Pamir Mountains are located. This highlighted their heritage, identifying them as being from the survival civilisations, and very likely an encrypted symbol indicating that they were descendants of refugees who chose to escape to the Himalayas and its periphery plateaus, post-great flood. Their geographical location in the Loess Plateau exposed them to the proximity, the expansion and rising of Saka to the north, in southern Central Siberia under the Tartar class-title system clusters that had just emerged.

This saw the Tartar warrior class-title system cluster features fused into those of the Teews', making the Teews a semi-warrior, semi-priest-merchant class-title system clusters, in particular, the reliance in Teew culture on military and the heavy use of mounted archery in its warfare. This would later evolve into horse-pulled-chariots that the Teews inherited from the last-cycle civilisation along with the arriving seafaring class title 'Jews', as well as the Yeniseian-Indo-European Ordos culture to its northwest, bringing technology contemporary to the western restoration civilisation in Europe and Africa that would also be integrated into the process of the voluntarily cultural merge with the merchant-priest class-title system clusters at the local mainland East Asian level, the Staon class-title group (their later successor known as Dzaeriryou), that stretched from coastal mainland East Asia, bordering the Teew south of southern Mongolia, after the former's conquest of the latter, a status quo that continued to fuel the push-and-pull effect between the two major global class-title systems post-last-cycle civilisations.

Prior to the Staon and Teew being drawn into the pull-and-push effect (which lasted roughly between 4000 – 3000 years ago), an earlier layer of the origin of the Staon people are their ancestral migrations from the Himalayan mountains and plateaus post-great flood to the Yangtze River Delta in different waves, a region sandwiched by great lakes, the Yangtze River, and the Pacific, becoming the founders of the Hmong–Mien, Kra–Dai and proto-Austronesian groups in that region. This is to be distinguished with the Austroasiatic group that had been inhabiting the south-eastern Himalayan periphery mountains (the upper Mekong, Salween and Irrawaddy basins) and expanding into the present-day Vietnamese coastline well before the great floods that brought down the last-cycle civilisation. The Bắc Sơn culture (12000 – 5000 BP) class-title where the Austroasiatic group originated from could also be the mother class-title to the later Kra–Dai class-title who migrated northward from northern coasts of mainland Southeast Asia into coastal mainland East Asia and became the ancestral group to the Great-Lake lower Yangtze and the Staon peoples.

The later emergence of the refugees in the Himalayan periphery mountains could have ventured north-eastern ward into the Great-Basin in mainland East Asia within the upper Yangtze River basin as well as eastward into coastal mainland Southeast Asia, becoming the ancestors to the proto-Austronesian group who would spread to coastal mainland East Asia,

Korean peninsula, southern islands of the Japanese archipelago and the Pacific islands.

The similarities regarding the material-designs in the cultures of the two proto-Austronesian subgroups stand out, with the arrival of one proto-Austronesian sub class-title in the Bali island (3000 BC) through the Philippines and Sulawesi on the one hand, and the other as the Dok class-title (corresponding to the Baodun and Three Star Mound cultures from 2700 - 1150 BC) led on the other hand, by the Gerdzaerirm Dzaeroong clan (Cancong). Features including protruding eyes, upward-curving fangs and mouths could be observed in the masks of Balinese Barong and the animal masks of Dok, whereas cloud-like patterns are featured in both of their costumes; best examples of a probable underlying connection between the sub-class-title system-clusters.

In the case of Teews' ancestral migrations, they followed a route from the Himalayan mountains and plateaus to Loess Plateau and further north of the mainland East Asian coastline, who would later be joined by the parts of the refugees of proto-Staon's ancestral settlements (Kra–Dai and Austronesian group) in the mid and lower Yangtze River great lakes region, following yet another episode of rising sea-level at a more local level.

The re-occurring sea-level rise events post-great flood was a norm during that epoch and in the case of the mid and lower Yangtze River great-lake regions, splitting the survivors who chose to stay in Yangtze River Delta from the refugees that chose to flee northward, following either the mainland East Asian coastline, or northwestern-ward to the Central Plain and Loess Plateau as mentioned.

Such northward migrations also exposed the forming Staon and the Teew sub-systems to the ever-expanding Sino-Tibetan and to a lesser extent Tibeto-Burman influxes of migrations coming from the Himalayan and its periphery mountains (roughly for an epoch between 5000 – 4000 years ago, the starting point being roughly from 6700 years after the conclusion of the great-flood epoch coinciding the Younger Dryas) to the west and southwest, the upper Mekong, Salween and Irrawaddy basins, respectively, which could be seen as another set of later waves of refugees coming out of hiding in the plateaus and mountains post-great flood. This would further flash away the distinct system-cluster features that had further formed on top of the inherited ones from the last-cycle civilisation among ancestral settlements of proto-Staon and partially the proto-Teew in the lower Yangtze River great lakes regions, with the later Staon holding on to these previous features for much longer.

This layer of diminishing memories to the previous class-title identity could explain the notable difference between Teews' mixed outlook as class-title system clusters and those of the Staon's with the Teews inability to grasp the Germro shamanism or wizardry shamanism, in the Staon's priest-feature, the scapulimancy, or bone divination. The Teew dismissed such practices as outlandish superstition that got in the way of class-title system clusters development, with semi-spiritual culture such as, Lek Klereong the Book of Changes, surviving as a product of a 'refining campaign', with philosophy and more graspable prophecy tools based off a digit-possibility system that draws cosmic-energy being its form, distinguishing it from its previous bone divination spirituality form where the cracks could have been those energy-drawing, digit-based possibilities; with ancestral worshipping reduced to mere formality, instead of its previous purpose that aimed to connect to spirituality and shamanism. Similarly after the Teew conquest of the Staon, face-tattooing was also dismissed as being backward.

This is another indication of the Saka class-title system clusters influence on the Teews, first through the Indo-European Afanasievo culture and later the Yeniseian-Indo-European Ordos culture, that accelerated the loss of understanding and mastery of spirituality in mainland East Asia. Given the Teew's foundational influence on the class-title system clusters in the region. This was despite a later Renaissance of the Staon's successor, Dzariryou, that almost overtook and re-absorbed the Teews' successor Dzaeen, whose name 'Dzaeen' would be recorded through Sanskrit as 'Cīna', in the ancient Greek language, as 'Thin' and the later Latin record of 'Sin' back into the priest-merchant class-title system clusters, but that status quo was short-lived as the Dzaeen overtook the Dzariryou at the end of this episodic class-title system clusters rivalry. Another subtle layer of the system-cluster dynamic within the merchant priest itself, in addition to the extensive Teew-Staon, Dzaeen-Dzariryou episodic rivalry was that both system clusters perceived the merchant-priest system clusters in the Austronesian-Kra–Dai region (and Jomon-Japonic with Staon's further north expansion to the Yellow Sea Bay-Three Peninsulas region) of the great lake area near the Yangtze River Delta, later the States of the Ongwoera and Woaat (Wu and Yue), as well as the Kra–Dai-Hmong–Mien region in the central Yangtze River basin, later the State of Sreal (Ch'u) as backward, due to the catastrophic destructions the above-mentioned sea level rises had in two locations of the Yangtze River basins, leading to stagnated development.

Yet such perceptions of the Teew and Staon regarding their southern neighbours came, again, from a lack of the knowledge, one that would otherwise allow them to recognise that their own civilisations came partially from the refugees of Austronesian, Kra–Dai and Hmong–Mien regions, fleeing the local sea-level rise and lake level rise in lower and mid Yangtze River basin as well as the encroachments of the Sino-Tibetan and Tibeto-Burman speaking migration groups, possibly forcing them to either self-assimilate into, or false-self-assimilate into the new dominating-group to buy time and wait for a later timing, usually spanning generations, for resistance in that scenario. The reflections of such events could be found in records depicting constant rivalry between Teew and the 'southern neighbours', and the Staon and 'southern neighbours', respectively, which somehow kept showing up, haunting them as if they had long inhabited the northern lands.

This could be seen as new sub-systems-clusters emerging from the northerly presence of the Austronesian Kra–Dai-Hmong–Mien and Jomon-Japonic (the Rooes-Teroong Liryou included in this continuum) class-title merchant-priest system-clusters receiving refugees from their southern branches, forcing Renaissance and reformations to rise, in the form of the newly-born Teew and Staon system-clusters.

Two other possibly scenarios that could have played out as the different aspects of the last-cycle civilisation inheritance came flooding in, along with the burden such an influx of people put on the capacity of resource harnessing, are one, Staon and Teew supporting their cousin system-cluster coming from the south under the direction of helping build the forming Teew and Staon sub-system-clusters; two, the arriving migrations from the south helping build the sub-system-cluster with the Teews, while putting more effort into promoting the last-cycle civilisation and Yangtze River basin identity that were still present among the Staon, than they did helping the Staon form the new sub-system-cluster.

This would serve as factors that pushed the newly-formed Teew and Staon, with partial support from their neighbours, the northernly presence of the Austronesian and Kra–Dai-Hmong–Mien speaking system-clusters for the reasons mentioned, to incorporate even more revolutionary system-clusters from the Tartar Saka, or in the case of the latter, incorporating more Germro Shamanism to try and enhance mental and physical ability from spirituality as solutions, or in seizing the opportunity to restore as much as the last-cycle civilisation cultures, while perceiving the already present merchant-priest class-title system-clusters in the north of mainland East Asia as leftovers, namely, the proto-Teroong Gehera and Seewkdeens system-clusters that somehow rivalled them.

The Saka class-title system clusters, the eastern branch of the rising Tartaria (with Scythians and Sarmatians in the west, forming their own Tartar class-title union) and its influence on the Teews could be seen in the later Hakka class-title system clusters, their obscure original remnant of the Teews influence and many other layers of a further push-and-pull effect down the path. The Hakka class-title system clusters had emerged as resilient and hardy, warrior-like people. Records depict them as 'migration waves' not subdued by any surrounding forces. They were geniuses in defence warfare and civil-military fusion. Their status as prominent merchants is a result of the absorption of the priest-merchant class-title system clusters in mainland East Asia (when features from such system clusters were still influential enough to delay its gravitation towards a shadow Tartar region) and the unshakable influence their ancestral Teews inherited from the Saka class-title system clusters.

Another Tartar class-title system cluster successor that inherited the name Saka was the Turkic-speaking Sakha who self-designated the Sakha title and who were originally semi-Tartar class-title system clusters described by the neighbouring Tungusic-Evenk semi-Tartar class-title in central Siberia as, Yako. The linguistic difference, and even any loss in translation would not be enough to explain the word change from Yako to Sakha. This appears to have been a rather deliberate 'sound corruption' by the Sakha Tartar class-title system clusters that were based roughly in the same Siberian region.

With their settlement in central Siberia between the 9th and the 16th century, overlapping with that of the Hakka migration period, the Sakha added another Tartar class-title system clusters influence on the southwardly migrating Hakka, with the aim of them joining the Hakka, both on the shared phonetic feature of the class-title system clusters name and cultural features, as well as physically joining them in the southward migration. This was in addition to the influence of the Tartar class-title features the Hakka inherited from the Teews, which in turn came from the earlier Saka class-title.

Card Kerrep Sewl I-8

Why are similar linguistic features of language spread out on the globe?

What is there to be perceived when convergent evolution is looked through as one of many, instead of the sole possible cause?

Linguistic Similarities between Languages Spoken throughout the Eastern and Western Coastal / Insular Branch of the Restoration Centres of the Survival Civilisation

The linguistic sources were studied, available for ten different languages that were spoken by the merchant-priest class title system clusters across Arctic Europe, Arctic North Asia, coastal mainland East Asia, northeast Asia, the Pacific northwest of North America, the south-eastern corner of North America on the Mexican Gulf shore, and Central America.

Some were reconstructed protoforms and some in contemporary form. These were categorised into 3 groups based on the phonetic similarities of the languages:

- Merchant-priest class-title system clusters A
- Merchant-priest class-title system clusters B
- Tartar-influenced semi-merchant-priest class-title system clusters

Finnish, Inuit, reconstructed ancient Japanese, Ainu, and Mayan would belong to group A. The reconstructed Staon language, Proto-Austronesian, the Yeniseian Ket, and Texan Indigenous Coahuilteco would belong to group B.

The need to use reconstructed or proto-languages is because some languages in the group lie in the region where constant waves of migration from the Tartar class-title system clusters poured in. In the push-and-pull effect, many lost the common linguistic features they had possessed as a common heritage from the last-cycle civilisations, such as the Japanese, and mainland East Asian languages possibly because of a geographical spread across a massive ocean with scattered islands, where geographical isolation dominated the fast-charged diversion of language evolution, as seen in the Austronesian languages; or linguistic islands and oceans, with the 'oceans' effectively altering, linguistically-engineering the 'islands', as could be observed in most cases.

The most obvious phonetic features in the first group are the constant use of suffixes. These consisted of a consonant and the vowel 'a', 'i', or 'o'; with vowel followed by 't', 'k', 's', 'r', 'n', or 'm' as another set of common suffixes. Lastly, a lengthened vowel, or lengthened consonant in the middle of words in some of the languages in this group was observed. Such examples can be seen in Finnish, Inuit, reconstructed ancient Japanese, Ainu, and Mayan respectively, listed in order below:

Finnish

Suffix set 1.   *sa, *la, *va, *ka, *ta, *to, *ki, *ti

Suffix set 2.   *et, *at, *ut, *us, *an, *en, *on, *un

Lengthened vowels and consonants in the middle.   *aa, *uu, *ii, *ee, *oo, *nn, *tt, *kk, *ll

Inuit

Suffix set 1.   *ga, *ma, *ta, *na, *pa, *ni

Suffix set 2.   *it, *ik, *uq, *us

Lengthened vowels and consonants in the middle. *uu, *ii, *mm, *nn, *tt, *kk, *pp, *ss, *vv

Reconstructed ancient Japanese

(simulation to a slightly Tartar class-title system clusters influenced Jomon; this happened as the once archipelago-peninsula stretching Jomon class-title system clusters were displaced by the Koreanic Tartar class-title system clusters migrants, ancestral to contemporary Korean people, and progressively pushed then further eastward across the sea, back into the Japanese archipelago)

Suffix set 1.   *na, *ka, *ca, *ci, *ri, *no, *po,

Suffix set 2.   *ut, *ur, *ar, *nir, *tir, *kir, *pir, *tor, *irm

Lengthened vowels and consonants in the middle.   Absent

Ainu
Suffix set 1.   *to, *ro, *da, *ka, *ga, *ki, *ni
Suffix set 2.   *st, *ok, *ak, *as, *ur, *or, *on
Lengthened vowels and consonants in the middle.   *tt, *kk,

Mayan
Suffix set 1.   *so, *no, *lo *to
Suffix set 2.   *ic, *ac
Lengthened vowels and consonants in the middle.   *uu, *oo, *aa

The most obvious phonetic features in the second group is the constant use of the sounds 'ir' and its variants as well as 'ong' in suffixes, with two-consonant forming a cluster as another suffix set. Additionally, 'qa'(and its variants), 'ong' (and its variants), 'ts' and 'dz' are the most common features in prefixes. One notable exception is the constant use of consonant clusters as prefixes in the Staon reconstructed language. The linguistic examples of the languages in group two will be demonstrated in order of reconstructed language Staon, Proto-Austronesian, Ket, and the Coahuilteco language:

Staon
Suffix set 1.   *ir, *irk, *ong, *oong, *irong
Suffix set 2.   *ks, *ws, *wk
Prefix   *qa, *ong, *ts, *dz
Consonant cluster prefix   *mr, *mp, *mper, *mtse,
                             *nk, *nker, *np,   *npre, *nper,
                             *st, *sq, *sm,   *smer, *sr,
                             *tn, *tk, *tq,
                             *km, *kmer *kr

Proto-Austronesian
Suffix set 1.   *irk, *irn, *irm, *ird, *irp, *ong, *oong
Suffix set 2.   Absent
Prefix   *qa, *iong

Ket
Suffix set 1.   *tir, *tirs*, birs
Suffix set 2.   *ks
Prefix   *qa

Coahuilteco

Suffix set 1.	*Absent*
Suffix set 2.	**pt*
Prefix	**tz, *gua*

Languages can change within a few generations as a result of the push-and-pull effects constantly present among class-title systems and this is a significant consideration for the effect between class-title systems common identity of the priest-merchant class-title system clusters to be preserved, or at least prolonged in the face of degeneration, however vague.

Where there are fewer features within two language groups the languages share would indicate the migration, or the isolation effect, which would render the Mayan language the most loosely tied to group one, given that the Jomon language is reconstructed. Otherwise Japanese could be as distant to the linguistic group as Mayan, in this case.

The Coahuilteco language would be in a similar situation in group two to Mayan in group one, given that the Staon language is also reconstructed. Otherwise, in this case, the mainland East Asian language (a mostly Tartar language, with very few previous priest-merchant class-title system clusters linguistic features left, in its dying 'dialects') would be the one most distant in relation to the other languages in group two.

The phonetic features in the Aztec language suggests its place within semi-Tartar, semi-priest-merchant class-title system clusters, tilting slightly more towards the latter because of their cultural merge with Mayan. This was similar to the Teew cultural merge with Staon. The Aztec suffixes: *pa, *la, *ma, *ya, *se, *ca, *ti, *li would look reminiscent of the features in group one, with sounds such as *xi, *chi, *qui being Tartar influence, which could be found in Tungusic, Mongolic languages as well as shadow Tartar language such as the one in mainland East Asia.

Card Kerrep Sewl I-9

Why was the one-piece robe a shared costume feature among the many class-title system clusters under merchant-priest and Tartar?

What does the shared cloud-like geometric patterns on the one-piece robe designs symbolise?

Similarities in Costumes, and Art Style throughout the Eastern and Western Coastal / Insular Branch of the Survival Civilisation

The one-piece robe, with curled-smoke and cloud-like geometric patterns on it, was widespread through different locations that mostly belonged to the restoration centres eastern branch, particularly the utmost similarity between the Aniu and the Alaskan Taku, Pacific northwest Tlingit class-title system clusters continuum, with the slight difference of an add-on cloak integrated into the one-piece robe for wear in Arctic and sub-arctic locations.

The Staon class-title system clusters had close, similar artistic patterns on their one-piece robes. However, the patterns that did appear on their bronze helmets, weapons and cauldrons could qualify them as the Aniu-Taku-Tlingit continuum, forming class-title system clusters that were constantly in contact with one another from coastal mainland East Asia, archipelago Northeastern Asia, coastal eastern Siberia, all the way into Alaska and Pacific Northwest in North America.

The one-piece robe worn by the Tocharian class-title system clusters in Central Asia with its artistic patterns, could be grouped with the Staon class-title system clusters as a sub-group, with their pointy hats forming another sub-group being almost identical to the pointy hats that the Ainu wore.

The pointy hat feature along with the curled-smoke and cloud-like geometric patterns found in Scynthian and Saka Tartar class-title system clusters cultures on the other hand, was an inheritance from the last-cycle civilisations before it emerged as new, completely different class-title system clusters. The curled-smoke and cloud-like geometric patterns were depictions of accessing higher dimensions during shamanistic practises.

The Wankarani and its successor class-title system clusters in the Andean ranges, (both are possibly successor cultures of the earlier Monte Verde culture, dating back to 18500 BP) was relatively distant to the four class-titles system clusters, mentioned above, with their use of rectangular shaped hats. This style formed a sub-group with the Staon class-title system clusters who wore slightly taller rectangular hats.

Card Kerrep Sewl I-10

Why were mythological features shared among different branches of the merchant-priest class-title system-clusters?

What did the widespread serpent-worshipping symbolise?

What did the widespread sun-worshipping symbolise?

What connections do the two forms of worshipping have?

In what sense could mythologies record the gradual distortion and corruption of itself?

Religion Similarities throughout the Eastern and Western (to a lesser extent) Coastal / Insular Branch of the Survival Civilisations

Snake-worshipping, Sun-worshipping, Face and Body Tattooing

Serpent-worshipping across the merchant-priest class-title system clusters in coastal America, East Asia, South East Asia and Europe is the active element in many earlier shamanisms — a reflection of the serpent guardian in the higher dimension when accessing Agartha.

Early forms, not so distant from the collapse of the last-cycle civilisation centres, were true reflections as knowledge of spirituality and consciousness were enhanced with hallucinogenic herbs used to access higher dimensional realms as practices that later corrupted into a symbol of deity in animalism and then even later, as mere formality.

There are records in merchant-priest class-title system clusters restoration centres globally, from the Hopi of Arizona (snake as wind and tempest-making, weather god), the Maya and Aztec, pre-Incan south American Chavín culture, Mapuche mythology in Chile, Nagas in Hindu mythology and to a lesser extent the European northern restoration centre in Prussian mythology where snakes were kept to feed the Prussian gods, West Africa in present-day Benin, Dogon religion (central Mali) where Lebe is believed to be the reincarnation of the first Dogon ancestor, who was resurrected in the form of a snake, the worshipping of Nral Kwroerl, literally meaning 'The Spiralling Femininity', a humanoid goddess with a snake-based body in mainland East Asian mythology, Austronesian-speaking and peninsular-archipelago Jomon people and to a lesser extent among the Ainu.

Face-tattooing was closely practised with shamanism and snake-worshipping and could be found in Staon merchant-priest class-title system clusters, Pacific Austronesian (especially on the forehead), Inuit, Jomon-Ainu (especially around the mouth), Métis, Tlingit, Alaskan Taku, with the tattooing among Mayan, Aztec, Incan, Chickasaw, Iroquoians, and Egyptian, often adorning other areas of their bodies.

Body tattooing was also found in the rising Saka-Scythian Tartar class-titles system clusters as cultural remnants (reasons as to why they emerged as a new Tartar class-title would be explored later) they also inherited from the last-cycle civilisations, or a partial re-absorption back into the priest-merchant class-title system clusters after emerging as new global class-title system cluster.

Sun worshipping was another shared practice among the global merchant-priest class-title system clusters, including the 26-sun god/deities in Filipino mythology, Swañco the sun goddess in Tocharian mythology, later partially absorbed into the Tartar class-title system clusters, and also partially absorbed into the priest-merchant class-title system clusters of the Hindu Kush Afghan region; their descendants were the fair skinned, light-eyed north-western-European-looking Nuristanis, Pashtuns, Kalash and Tajiks, all of whom are partially influenced by the Yeniseian and Turkic groups genetically speaking. More examples of the sun-worshipping phenomena are to be found in the Ainuric Chup Kamui in Ainu, Inti in Incan mythology, Antu in Mapuche mythology, Akycha in Inuit mythology, Tonatiuh, god of the Sun and ruler of the heavens in Aztec mythology, Yhi, an Australian Wotjobaluk aboriginal Karraur goddess of sun, light and creation, Gnowee, an Australian aboriginal solar goddess who searches daily for her lost son, by the light of her 'torch' the Sun and finally the Tama-nui-te-ra in Māori mythology.

Similar to snake-worshipping, it was originally a reflection of the inner core of Earth, the deepest layer of Agartha where the duck-headed entities exist, in both the seventh and the eighth dimension or the extra-terrestrial coyote entity in the eighth dimension and several dimensions up. These were a reminder of the need for spirituality and consciousness mastery to pass the trial on Earth and get closer to them (explored in later chapter), before they corrupted into the simplified idea of the energy providing sun.

Among all these cases of sun-worshipping, Gnowee the son-searching sun-goddess is a good example of where the gradual process of corruption into formality was captured and integrated into the mythology. The sun-torch is the symbol of the duck-headed humanoid (who created the trial for Homo sapiens to pass so that they could access Agartha) and coyote entities, both of whom serve as a motivation for Homo sapiens to re-discover or hold on to its lost 'son' — the knowledge of consciousness, spirituality and DNA mastery that was slowly being lost after the last-cycle civilisation collapse.

The snake-worshipping and sun-worshipping, face-tattooing and body-tattooing that was common among the merchant-priest class-title system clusters, would signal the common class-title heritage inherited from the last-cycle civilisations, while also maintaining constant contact with one another through seafaring technology. Although this was based on a non-mechanic-based science, for example, a combination of bioengineering and telepathy with sea creatures who were used as 'ships', with sea monsters recorded in mythology being reflective of such different science, albeit with mechanic-based science era connotations, where the monsters were depicted as disruptive or evil, before being corrupted into a less advanced version of its previous self.

Reference:

i. Cartes tartares and La dynastie tartare by Didier Lacapelle

Card Kerrep Sewl I-11

Why are floods a shared theme among world mythologies?

What would ancient refugee waves have looked like in the epoch of the great flood, or great sea level rise?

What do legendary civilisation centres have to do with all these?

What is behind the legendary coat of these civilisations?

Three Possible Centres of the Last-cycle Civilisation Where All Class-titles System Clusters and Ethnic Groups were Well-connected and the Escape Routes from them in Proximity to Relative, or Absolute Highlands

Escape Routes Following the Drastic Rise of Sea Levels, (circa 400 metres)

Selected Geographic Escape Locations of the **Western Centre of Last-cycle Civilisation Atlantis:**

The islands that were originally Moroccan, Tunisian, the Alps, the Carpathian and Scandinavian mountains; the eastern side of the Rocky mountains, Iceland, Labrador, Greenland, sub-Arctic, the coast of Canada along the North-western Passage and Hudson Bay, the eastern side of the mountains in Central America and the eastern side of Andes.

Selected Geographic Escape Locations of the **Central Centre of Last-Cycle Civilisation Kumari Kandam (Lemuria) Located in the Central/ Southern Indian Ocean:**

The landing point here was Hindu Kush, the Tengri Tagh mountains, the Himalayan mountains, the Himalayan Bhö (བོད་, IPA: [pʰøʔʌ]), Iranian, Anatolian, the Arabian plateaus and the Ethiopian mountains.

Selected Geographic Escape Routes of the **Eastern Centre of Last-cycle Civilisation, Sundaland Joined with Australia, Forming the Mu Continent:**

Australian western plateau, Australian eastern coastal mountains, the eastern side of the Himalayan Bhö and Mongolian plateaus, the island of the original Manchurian shore, as well as the island of the original Korean Mt. Paektu, Kamchatka and its neighbouring Sea of Okhotsk shores, Alaskan coast, west coast of North America to the western side of Rocky mountains, and the western sides of the Central American mountains, and the Andes.

* There may well have been alternate escape routes as not all survivors decided to head towards the closest highlands. Those from Atlantis, for example, could have decided to flee to the Hindu Kush, and those from Mu may also have decided to flee to the Hindu Kush, or Madagascar instead of the elevated coastal areas of the Western pacific, or Australia, even although they were closer.

Card Kerrep Sewl I-12

Why did cultural-layer rich Himalayan Central Branch Restoration civilisations play minor roles in the world historically?

Why did other, more influential civilisations, choose to land in the Himalayan in case of contingencies?

Why is the legendary Agartha often associated with Himalayan civilisations? What is the connection between the Himalayan mountains, its periphery plateaus and the Tengri Tagh mountains?

The Fading Importance of the Central Branch Restoration, Relinquishing its Role to the Eastern and Western Branch Restoration

The central branch 'restoration' civilisation was overtaken by the eastern and the western branch restoration as the descendants of the eastern branch in particular ventured into mainland East Asia from the Himalayan Bhö plateau, or the Arctic Siberia base after the sea level drop, while the western branch restoration established itself mainly in Northern Europe, the European Mediterranean shores, Northwest Africa and the coast of the Americas. This happened as the lowland area offered more resources than the Himalayan Bhö plateau and followed a trajectory where Himalayan Bhö optimised the dividends of its intensely elevated geography and exploded into a powerhouse to be reckoned with and recorded for a relatively short-period of time, corresponding with the efforts of kings Tagri Nyensig and Namri Songtsen (570-620 AD) to unify the plateau. Epochs of twilight eras would then follow after the outbreak of civil wars on the plateau after 842 AD, giving the rise to de-centralised valley-based-powers.

In more recent history, as Tartaria dissolved under Slavic expansion into Siberia, most of the Tartar class-title system clusters holders fled to Himalayan Bhö. This transformed Himalayan Bhö from an already Tartar influenced central branch restoration centre, to a shadow Tartar region with significant priest-merchant cultural leftover features that were found in its spiritual traditions, with more recent versions of central and eastern continental Siberian-styled Tartar shamanism/Tengrism added to its original priest-merchant shamanism, and what had been absorbed from early Tartar expansion.

That said, the older layers of the culture, such as the Bardo Thodol, or Himalayan Bhö Book of Dead, a culmination of pre-historic Himalayan Bhö religion Yungdrung Bon (founded by Tonpa Senrab Miwoche, 16017 BCE), which had its own version of shamanism similar to a much more ancient Siberian shamanism that was common immediately following the receding of the great flood, in Arctic coastal Siberia and practices in Americas, remaining in essence 'restoration'.

This could be an indicator of the Central branch refugees from **Kumari Kandam** (**Lemuria**) using the Himalayan Bhö Plateau and Tengri Tagh mountains as a transitory base to allow further advances into the coastal Arctic in Siberia, before crossing into North America, using sea faring technology.

This could also be because the Himalayan Bhö Plateau and Tengri Tagh mountains were already a settled, periphery area of the Central branch last-cycle civilisation pre-great-flood that occurred between 12,900 to 11,700 years ago and corresponds with the Younger Dryas. These regions were chosen as places that would develop spirituality a long time before waves of refugees from the spirituality-focussed last-cycle civilisation, in this case mostly from **Kumari Kandam**, arrived during the great flood epoch and made their own contribution to Yungdrung Bon culture.

The Central branch of the last-cycle civilisation **Kumari Kandam** was the most well-connected with Agartha of the three branches, with Mu and Atlantis following its lead. Hollow Earth is also symbolic, with the lava-filled crests and mantles as 3-dimensional physical covers for dimensional-shifting spaces within planet Earth, either vertically into higher dimensions, or horizontally into a parallel universe within a three-dimensional reach of the alternate, yet in essence the similar planet Earth (we will explore this more in **Card Kerrep Lerats IV**).

Another similar case is the Yeniseian class-title system-clusters, likely already present in the Lake Baikal-Tengri Tagh regions for at least 10,000 years before the start of the global-scale great flood from 12,900 to 11,700 BP, yet were joined by the refugees, the Central Kumari Kandam last-cycle civilisation who chose Tengri Tagh mountain islands as their shelter as well as with the inflowing North American Na-Dene-speaking groups primarily in the sub-Arctic area of North America, with Tlingit, Athabaskan-Eyak being few notable examples.

Proposed theory of the North American makeup of the Yeniseian class-title system-clusters being a reverse migration from earlier groups having crossed the Bering Strait could be seen as the Na-Dene group having migrated out of Siberia around 20,000 BP and settled in North America shortly afterwards, before migrating back to Siberia. The reverse migration took place during the great-flood era where their migration destinations were the Tengri Tagh mountain island as well as further north on the Arctic coast of Siberian northern extreme, further contributing to the forming of a proto-Yeniseian class-title system-clusters with heavy Kumari Kandom influences, given the refugees are in high-tiers in the trial system as well as how the Lake Baikal-Tengri Tagh-Himalayan-Hindu Kush regions were already viewed by Kumari Kandam as an extensive periphery continuum of themselves addition to Antarctica long before the great-flood.

Early forms of Tengrism, spirituality-based cymatic technology and traditions, and mega lifts used for vertical agriculture purposes tied to the spirituality-science, already being possessed, harnessed and partially mastered by the proto-Yeniseian class-title is an indicator of the integral status of the regions to Kumari Kandam. Yet with the Na-Dene-speaking groups reverse migrating into the proto-Yeniseian class-title territories, a lesser extent of Mu and Atlantis influences were added to the already-present Kumari Kandam ones. (which will be explored in **Card Kerrep Sewl V-1**).

As the proto-Yeniseian class-title system-clusters came out of hiding to resettle the neighbouring Lake Baikal region, as they had done pre-great-flood epochs, they have also transited into the Yeniseian class-title, before rising to a regional superpower to be reckoned with and recorded. They have done so via forming a class-title system-clusters coalition with the Turkic-Mongolic Kuahong Nera-led Tartar class-title system-clusters, along with the Indo-European Saka class-title and Tocharian class-title as well as the proto-Tungusic class-title such as the Seewkdeens which was partially a reunion with their genetic cousins. This would have to do with the previous spread of proto-Na-Dene sub-class-title further sub-splitting when reaching the eastern extreme, the northern Pacific shores of Siberia, forming a southward influx to join the ancient north east Asians who were Japonic-Jomon in northern to southern Manchuria, contributing the first wave of ancestors to the proto-Turkic group, with the second being flows of Yeniseian from the Lake Baikal who, upon contact with the northward expanding Seewkdeens Tungusic group from Manchuria at around 3500 BC, were perhaps reminded of their settled proto-Turkic genetic and cultural cousin groups stretching from the Amur River basin to southern Manchuria and migrated south to join them, contributing another Yeniseian sub-stratum to the southern Manchurian cultures who were the proto-Turkic class-title well until 150 BC.

Both of the above-mentioned flows of the proto-Yeniseian / Yeniseian group could have also flowed into the Ainuric group in Armur River Basin and the Jomon-Japonic groups in southern Manchuria and southern Mongolian Plateau. This would explain two phenomena, one genetically and another culturally-linguistically.

The shared genetic substratum underlying the Na-Dene, Turkic, and Yeniseian class titles contributes to their observed Eurasian appearances, often being described as resembling the contemporary Turkic-speaking states in Central Asia.

This was already the case before the later influx from the easternmost centre of eneolithic Indo-European Afanasievo culture class-title into the Yeniseian and the proto-Turkic groups; with Afanasievo culture class-title being the descendents of the pre-great-flood Afontova Gora class-title (c. 18,000–12,000 BP) where the genetic blond hair feature first emerged on top of the already present pale-skin, producing the later highly distinguishable appearances of Afanasievo culture group and the much later Tocharians, Sakas and Gava-Sogdians.

The more detailed origin of the Afanasievo culture class-title itself and inter-relationships with closely-related groups would be that of the cousin migration culture contemporaneous of the Yamanaya coming out of hiding from the Caucasus Mountains, settling the Pontic–Caspian steppe at around 3300 BC, thereby splitting with the Afanasievo culture class-title who continued to migrate eastward. In this sense, both the Yamnaya and Afanasievo cultures were the descendant groups of the pre-great-flood Afontova Gora class-title (c. 18,000–12,000 BP) previously having fled the great-flood from the lower Yenisei River Basin to the Caucasus Mountains, with Afanasievo later reverse migrating to the same region in the lower Yenisei River Basin, despite being 12,600 years apart from their ancestral Afontova Gora group.

However, the two class-titles of Yamanaya and Afanasievo cultures did not simply come out of hiding from the mountain islands / mountains, but emerged as semi-nomadic class-titles with low flexibility for new sub-class-titles to emerge; a similar case would be some of Yamanaya group's descendant class-titles such as the Sintashta and its later Vedic form of class-title, famous from its 'caste' class-title system-clusters prompting the later rise of Saka and Scythian as first Tartar class-titles to intensify the nomadic-apects of life and enormously increased flexibility for new sub-class-titles to emerge, forming a fluctuating yet equilibrated state of relative egalitarianism distinguished and powerful enough to rival the merchant-priest class-title system clusters.

In the case of the Na-Dene class-title, it has possibly absorbed much later post-great flood waves of the Indo-European Afanasievo culture class-title migrating to sub-Arctic North America, adding to their own already Eurasian-looking appearances. One branch of the Na-Dene class-title who settled in sub-Arctic North America at around 10,000 BP were later named by their linguistic and genetic neighbouring cousin Tlingit on the western coast of the same area as Tahltan, indicating an earlier start of the push-and-pull effect between the the merchant-priest class-title system-clusters and the Tartar one when compared with Eurasia, with Tlingit remaining the former class-title system-clusters and Tahltan tilting to the latter despite their shared beliefs of sun and sky gods inherited from the last-cycle civilisation.

Such Indo-European influxes particularly into the Yeniseian and the proto-Turkic group, in one way, would contribute the genetic subgroups with less obvious features of light eye and hair colours among the previously mentioned Nuristanis, Pashtun, Kalash and Tajik people still present in Central Asia and the Hindu Kush areas.

On the other hand, such Indo-European class-title push-and-pull merges with the Yeniseian and the proto-Turkic ones would also contribute to the latter's genetic subgroup who were historically recorded to have light eye, hair colours and pale skins, an even more Caucasian-looking, during the later epochs of Yeniseian expansion in Bronze age, either by themselves, or via the Kuahong Nera coalition. The same applies to the Yeniseian substratum in the proto-Turkic groups whose expansions during the Kuahong Nera coalition era and the much later ones in late antiquity times resulting in a semi-Turkic takeover in mainland East Asia.

All of these distinguished physical features in additional to their class-title ones left their remarks in historical records particularly because of the

Yeniseian and proto-Turkic / Turkic groups' clashes with mainland East Asian powers.

Lastly, the observed geographic schizophrenia of the proto-Turkic class-title torn between Manchuria and the Tengri Tagh and their physical appearance highly resembling the North American Na-Dene class-titles could both be traced back to the class-title's proto-Yeniseian and proto-Na-Dene origins; and the same applies after the Indo-European merge with them as all three class-title groups experienced such merges in different times.

As to the enigma of the Caucasian physical features among the Ainuric class-title (still present today as the Aniu people) and the ancient Jomon-Japonic class-title, the previously mentioned proto-Yeniseian / Yeniseian, proto-Turkic, Na-Dene reverse migration and the eneolithic Indo-European Afanasievo class title could have all contributed to the phenomenon.

As high-tier ruling elites within the system-clusters coalition, and with the leading Kuahong Nera sub-class-title possibly valuing the merchant-priest class-title elements the Yeniseian carried with them in a subliminal manner despite the ongoing heated rivalry between the two global class-tiles, the Yeniseian group saw their language rose to prestige (circa 3rd century BC–1st century AD), largely corresponding with the heyday of the Kuahong Nera class-title Confederation / Empire, partially ancestral to the later Hunnic Empire, geographically centred on the Mongolian Plateau and Lake Baikal. Additionally, the genetic cousin of the Yeniseian group, the Proto-Turkic group within the Proto-Turkic-para-Mongolic cluster, were one of the two clusters of ethnic cores (the other being Saka-Tocharian) within the Tartar Kuahong Nera coalition.

Yet the Yeniseian class-title's voluntary assimilation into the Tartar Kuahong Nera class-title system-clusters would begin to slowly reverse as their branch ventured into northern mainland East Asia around 250 years after the disintegration of the Kuahong Nera as a regional superpower and became known as the Kad, or Kyeot group, the same stem name inherited by the contemporary Ket people — this group had declined close to a millennia before the Slavic-Cossack expansion and retreated further north into the Yeniseian river basin briefly after the Slavic-Cossack expansion into Siberia arrived in the Yeniseian River-Lake Baikal region in the 17th century — in one of the southward migration waves of the Tartar class-titles into mainland East Asia between 304 – 316 AD.

The Yeniseian-Kad would be further drawn into the push-and-pull effects between the Tartar and the merchant-priest class-title system-clusters, the latter of whom had been declining, yet still relevant in mainland East Asia; and faced a massacre campaign where the non-Kad groups were mobilised through bounty hunting incentives (369 AD) to hunt heads of Kad-Caucasian-looking groups, schemed by an adopted son of the Kad group who was genetically non-Kad and of merchant-priest origin, named Nyeam Mrirnl (born as Daak Mrirnl, the son of Daak Rerirk, leader of the Kad), resulting in the decline of the Yeniseian-Kad in mainland East Asia within the next 300 years till the semi-Turkic, semi-merchant-priest class-title, Reeraong, or Dang / Tang takeover of mainland East Asia. The re-absorption of the Yeniseian-Kad back into semi merchant-priest class-title system clusters would only start after that, pushing them to spend their epochs of twilight times as Turkicised groups, possibly being amnesiac with their previous Yeniseian class-title natures.

Another Yeniseian class-title's branch would flee from the Mongolian Plateau and Lake Baikal region, westward with the northern Kuahong Nera and played crucial role in the building of the later Hunnic class-title empire (370s–469 AD) where they rose to power again. First in the Volga River basin, and later on the northern shore of Black Sea, Don River basin, Dnjepro River basin, central and eastern Donau River basin. Such regaining of the regional superpower status delayed the beginning of their re-absorption back into the merchant-priest class-title system-clusters, which only began after the collapse of the Hunnic class-title. One branch of such a Yeniseian group post-Hunnic class-title empire collapse would first be absorbed into the other remnants of the Hunnic class-title groups of Turkic-Mongolic origins, and later, with new incoming waves of Turkic migrations from Central Asia (a butterfly effects caused by the semi-Turkic class-title takeover of mainland East Asia) formed a class-title system-clusters of their own, giving birth to the Hungarian conquest of the Carpathian Basin in 895 AD. From that, this branch of Yeniseian elites were able to solidify a newly-formed Hungarian class-title system-clusters through further cooperating with and having the local Magars already in the Hungarian basin assimilated into them.

However, this group of Yeniseian elites, with the local Magars, the newly-arrived Turkic and the older-layered Turkic groups they had worked with since the Kuahnong Nera-Hunnic times, would together become minority given their proximity to all the Slavic-speaking class-title system-clusters migration influxes, giving birth to the hybrid outlook of the new Hungarian class-title system clusters. A class-title with a majority of Slavic gene-makeup, minority Yeniseian, Tocharian-Saka (which could be seen as a reverse migration of a Indo-European sub-class-title group back into the Indo-European Slavic-dominated regions), Turkic and Magars gene-makeup, speaking a Uralic language — which the Yeniseian group elites might have 'reform-adopted', following the disintegration of the Hunnic class-title empire when their own Yeniseian language lost prestige — with Yeniseian linguistic remnants as well as the new Magar and the Slavic influences all incorporated into it. As a new class-title system-clusters, they would quickly tilt back and self-integrate into the merchant-priest system-clusters in Central Europe.

Such case of linguistic-demographic combination was similar to that observed in the earlier heyday of the Kuahong Nera class-title power in southern Central Siberia where the genetic makeup of the population core was possibly Saka-Tocharian and Turkic-Mongolic, with minority Yeniseian mixture. This was a result of the Saka-Tocharians arrivals to the Lake Baikal area in large numbers of migrations from Tengri Tagh, Pamir-Hindu Kush (where their Indo-European ancestors' eastward migration in turn started from the Caucasus); the proto-Turkic from Tengri Tagh and Arctic coast of northern Siberia; and the proto-Mongolic from the Tengri Tagh and Himalayan mountains / plateaus. With the Saka-Tocharian and Turkic-Mongolic having become the demographic majority of the Kuahong Nera class-title, the class-title as whole, however, chose to adopt the Yeniseian language to be part of the prestige, best demonstrated in the language's use among the Yeniseian higher-tier aristocratic sub-class-title within the Kuahong Nera class-title system-clusters.

It is observed in both case of the later developments of the Yeniseian class-title group and the Himalayan Bhö — the latter of who also came possibly from the Central Branch last-cycle civilisation and took refuge from the Himalayan mountains and plateaus islands during the great flood, neighbouring the refugees of the proto-Yeniseian in Tengri Tagh mountain islands — that the same pattern of the short, concentrated explosion into a regional superpower to be reckon with, followed with rapid decline into epochs of twilight eras, either being re-absorbed into a merchant-priest class-title system-cluster, themselves becoming a semi-merchant-priest class-title system cluster, or being further flashed by the push-and-pull effects.

The self-involving essence (which will be explored in **Card Kerrep Sewl II-2** and **Card Kerrep Sewl II-5**) in both the Himalayan Bhö and the Yeniseian class-title groups' developments could be seen as their firm connections to Kumaria Kandam, long after fleeing it from the great-flood, and therefore being closer to the nature of Agartha, reflecting such essence in the form of their self-involving development patterns, as in always ending in a smaller scale of their previous selves and clinging onto that smaller status in the longer run. This is similar to the higher dimensions splitting from the lower-tier ones via self-involving into realms smaller than nanotechnology could reach. Developments in an outward-revolving manner, increasing in size and power in the three-dimensional world in the long run, does not apply to both the cases of the Himalayan Bhö and the Yeniseian class-title groups even long after their loss of meta-cognitions in such essence of themselves.

Card Kerrep Sewl I-13

Why were the Gosford Glyphs discovered in Australia?

Why was there a lack of writing systems in the Australian aboriginal civilisation and the Andean Inca civilisation?

What were the roles of writing systems in addition to general recording and communication?

The Discovery of Egyptian-styled Hieroglyphs (Gosford Glyphs) in Southeastern Australia.

Coming from Atlantis, the Moorish, from the south of the western restoration centre, contributed heavily to the establishment of the western branch restoration of the priest-merchant class-title system. The Phoenicians from the south of the western restoration centre were the sub-branch responsible for the spread of their 'Egyptian' hieroglyphs to Australia through their migration to that continent.

This more recent layer most likely added to the existing influence that the refugees from the central (Kumari Kandam in the Indian Ocean) and eastern (Mu in the Pacific, an extensive Australia), brought with them, or

Revoice - Uncurling The Involute Carrier of Reality

could even have come from the western centres immediately following the flood. However, it could have only ever been used by a limited range of class-titles, which, over time, faded away.

What's more likely, is that a writing system, contemporary with the spread of the Egyptian-styled hieroglyphs, passed from the eastern restoration centre to restoration Australia, and at some point, class-title system clusters were able to monitor or scan any writing scripts through telepathy — knowledge they inherited from one of the three centres, or in cooperation with the coyote entities — took advantage of the collapse of the last-cycle civilisation and then rose to power.

They could have imposed a set of rules on how the inhabitants of the Australian restoration centre should think. Using 'message sticks', as is known, the Australian aborigines had no writing systems, the restoration class-title groups in Australia used the vagueness in the symbolism that passed for artistic patterns to preserve their values and enjoyed a limited autonomy.

The same fate could have befallen the Incas where they used Quipu, knotted string devices that could pass for fabric manufacturing, to preserve their autonomy under a more spiritually-developed, yet corrupted overlord. In both cases, a lack of writing system could have been a result of the trade-off by the Australian and Andean restoration centre inhabitants, because of a voluntary abandonment of the writing system spread there, rather than a civilisational backwardness as it appeared on the superficial level.

Card Kerrep Sewl I-14

What are the connections between the Egyptian Theban legion and the Moors? Why is the supposedly East Asian black-and-white, Kuahroom-Laong-styled symbol in the Book of Changes found on Theban legion flouting?

The Multiple Layers of 'Fog' Names Coating the Western Branch of Survival Civilisation

A circle divided by black-and-white, Kuahroom-Laong-styled symbol, coined by Lek Klereong, otherwise known as Book of Changes, (supposedly East Asian symbolism) has a similar variant on the flouting of the Theban legion. It was led by St. Maurice/Moors, which could well be the sign of the Moorish seafaring technology that they inherited from the last-cycle civilisation western centre, Atlantis migrations to the eastern restoration branch, bringing this concept and symbol to East Asia, a common heritage both the western and eastern branch of restoration civilisation, inherited from the last-cycle civilisation, or alternatively, an influx of Mu-inherited eastern restoration centre influence through interactions.

Card Kerrep Sewl I-15

What could Athanasius Kircher's theory of the Egyptian hieroglyphs-oracle-bones-script imply?

Athanasius Kircher's theory of oracle bones script deriving from 'Egyptian' hieroglyphs, in a similar sense to the Kuahroom-Laong symbol, should be read as a sign of common heritage between the eastern and western branch of restoration centres from their last-cycle ancestral civilisation that showed the less explicit similarities between the two scripts Kircher spotted, with the oracle bones being a heritage from the eastern centre of the last cycle civilisation, the Mu continent, with possible mutual sharing and borrowing between the west and the east.

Card Kerrep Sewl I-16

Why do the Tamil-speaking Dravidians physically look like the Australian aborigines?

Why do the Dravidians and the Australian aborigines to some extent, physically resemble the Moorish?

Routes of East-ward Spreading of the Western Restoration Centre Hieroglyphs to Southern India and Australia

The Tamil-speaking Dravidians could have been descendants of the inter-mixing between dark-skinned Phoenicians/ancient Moorish and earlier prehistoric migration waves established there at the tip of South Asia (who were also dark-skinned), before further migrating to Australia, adding to the gene pool of the Australian Aborigines there, who were, genetically, cousins of the Dravidians through the prehistoric migration mentioned earlier, and possibly to New Zealand, either partially forming the Māoris, or adding to the layer of the locals' eastern restoration centre heritage as their own ancestors leapfrogged from Indonesia/Melanesia to New Zealand. This could be seen as routes where the Egyptian-styled hieroglyphs were brought to Australia, directly, or indirectly through Southern India.

Card Kerrep Sewl I-17

Why was there the lack of writing system in Northern Europe before the invention of Runic script?

Why is there such 'backwardness' in historic Northern Europe?

What was the role of the, by design, complex Egyptian hieroglyphs?

What were the roles of the Phoenician script and the Libyco-Berber alphabet?

What is an alternate means to archive information in addition to surfaces of smoothed-out materials?

The role of the Egyptian Hieroglyphs and the 'Lack of Writing System' in Northern Europe

Contemporary with the Egyptian-styled hieroglyphs where it was used to gain access to spirituality and superhuman ability, simplified variants of hieroglyphs systems, such as the Phoenician script and the Libyco-

Berber alphabet was rapidly developed for writing purposes as easier versions of the writing system designed for general communication that was lost from Atlantis, with only the one for spirituality (Egyptian hieroglyphs) remaining.

The lack of such for general communication before the development of the Runic writing system from Scandinavia was the result of the gradual loss of the know-how and technology that had been inherited from Atlantis as the Atlantis refugees fled to those northern islands to live with more primitive, periphery civilisations in the Scandinavian mountains. For some time, during the great flood, the Atlantis refugees became known as the first-generation enlightenment teachers in the Scandinavian mountain island. Such civilisation gaps between Atlantis refugees and the locals were quite hard, concerning know-how as technology might not have been fully understood, resulting in a partial loss down the generations.

There may have been advanced recording-technology such as telepathic archiving in minds (non-excavatable now), where such Phoenician-styled, simplified script was used in Northern Europe until the time that such script developed into Runic script, creating an illusion of the backwardness of the North. This is even more the case as materials, especially paper-like writing medians, are harder to preserve in the Scandinavian damp, wet, yet not quite the Siberian-styled rigidity where permafrost could be formed, than in the dry south where in Egypt's case, a telepathic archiving know-how (non-excavatable now) co-existed with the archiving on materialistic matters such as walls in the buildings, pottery and papyrus that was later excavated.

Card Kerrep Sewl I-18

Why is Finland considered the location of Troy and Sweden and the Baltic shores Greek-Achaeans?

Why does Canadian indigenous sub-arctic Cree syllabics resemble the Phoenician script and the Libyco-Berber alphabet?

What does the Viking / Varangian expedition into Greenland and North America symbolise?

Why were there disproportionately high frequency of wars and rivalries among ancient European civilisations?

Possible Multi-sub-centres within the Western Restoration Centres

Refugees who came out of hiding from the Scandinavian mountain island after the great flood would later spread through north-western Europe, all the way to the Arctic coast of Scandinavia and western Siberia to rival and border its southern restoration centre in Europe, which centres Spain, Morocco, Mali, the Alps and Anatolia (all islands during the great rise of sea level).

The Inuktitut syllabics and Cree syllabics as a whole, instead of being a creation of missionaries, could have had an ancient, shared heritage with either the Mu-based hieroglyphs brought with them through the Na-Dene migration from Siberia into North America before being simplified later, or an Atlantis-based one arriving from the Atlantis on coast of North America; or have been the result of ancient cultural exchange between restoration centres around sub-arctic Canadian coast / Greenland and Europe / north African restoration centres.

The Viking expedition along with the Phoenician expedition in this contexts could both have been a symbol of much more ancient interactions between the two coasts in the Northern Atlantic through the seafaring technology inherited from Atlantis, with the parallel being the Viking one from the northern branch of the western restoration centre as a re-occurring epoch following the earlier Phoenician one from the southern branch of the same restoration centre; and an effort to voluntarily migrate back to the American East coast to join the coastal cousins who had also descended from the last-cycle civilisation, which triggered the script exchange between the two coasts, its product being the similarity of the Cree syllabics to the Phoenician script and to a lesser extent the Viking Runic script. Finland, with its proximity to the Scandinavian mountains, later became Troy (Homer in the Bafticl by FeUce Vinci, where Troy was located in the village of Troija, between Helsinki and Turku; a caste rivalling, or sub-system rivalling existence that simultaneously kept the established Tartaria, or the Scythians at bay externally, a class-title system-clusters that coexisted with the southern sub-branch of the western restoration in Europe. Venice, the name sake of the 'Phoenicians', as all other class-title identities were, tolerant of slight phonetic variations in the class-title name and in this case its sub-branch at the mouth of River Po; this also applied to Morocco, Tunisia, Iberia, all within the Carthage sphere of influence. As restoration centres of the last-cycle civilisation, both the northern and the southern branches of the western restoration centre were separated from their East Asian, Southeast Asian as well as West coast America counterparts by Tartaria.

The Trojan war, in this sense, could be seen as class-title system clusters rivalry between the 'Trojans', who came out of hiding from the Scandinavian mountains much earlier than the 'Greek-Achaeans', who were the predecessors of the same warrior-merchant-priest class-title system clusters, in the Baltic, Scandinavian region. Similarly, later came the Vikings and Varangians, with both names referring to the class-title system clusters, instead of a homogenous ethnic group. This could be seen as rivalry limited to Northern Europe — the northern branch of the restoration centre in the west.

On the other hand, the Punic Wars, could have been symbolic in depicting the two rivalling restoration centres in Europe, with Troy-Rome (based in shores of Baltic Sea) being symbolic of the north (led by Scandinavians) and Carthage (based in shore of the Mediterranean Sea) being symbolic of the south (led by Phoenician/Moorish people).

Card Kerrep Sewl I-19

Why were there so many cultural similarities between the Carthage-based Phoenicians and the Venice-based Venetian merchants?

Why are there linguistic similarities among the class title, Phoenician, Venetian and Vandalic?

What was the motivation that pushed Viking / Varangian expeditions as far as the North American coast to the far west and the Caspian Sea to the far east?

Why are some portion of Venetians and Tunisian Berbers uncharacteristically fair-skinned and light-eyed?

Signs of Legacy and Later Successive Groups and Class-title System Clusters Assimilators

Carthage and Venice were later inherited by the Vandalic class-title system from the northern sub-branch, distinct from that of the Vikings-Varangians, being a result of the differences in how the former merged the merchant, warrior and priest elements into its class-title system, striking a balance through putting less or more stress on either of the three, culturally and ideologically adopting the existing merchant class-title system there, with genome remnants still seen in present-day Venice and the Berbers in Tunisia where faired-skin and light-eyed features can be found.

The later Vikings, Varangians, were the product of cooperative effort between the merchant and warrior class-title within the European system clusters (striking a different balance than did the Vandalic, giving rise to their difference in class-titles), or in the hiring of mercenaries from Tartary territory, before utilising their seafaring technology inherited from the western branch of survival civilisation to sail to the Caspian sea and even back to America, the intentions of which being either a potential countering and re-absorption campaign against the Tartar class-title to the northern and eastern coast of Caspian sea, an effort to migrate back to the American east coast voluntarily (mentioned earlier), or to offer aid to the North American merchant-priest class-title system-clusters against the Tartar counterparts also present there.

Card Kerrep Sewl I-20

What was the role of Morocco and Egypt in the merchant-priest class-title system-clusters?

Why would the United States of America, in its early stage, willing to pay tribute to the Moorish / Barbary?

Why did the United States of America and Moorish Morocco enter a series of cross-Atlantic interactions where 'rivalry' is insufficient to describe?

Moorish Connection with East Coast America as an Aspect of its Seafaring Role, Similar to that of Egypt's

Morocco is used as a forefront to connect to the east coast of the Americas (from Great Lakes, Iroquois to Argentina; it's not an absolute continuum as Tartarian influence could stretch from the sandwiched inland North America to portions of the east coast, cutting the north and south of the priest-merchant class-title in Atlantic shore of Americas) where Egypt, in the same fashion as Morocco, is also used as a base for seafaring. However, as opposed to Morocco, Egypt was, additionally, used for document archiving (archives in a storage system and old harbour were discovered on the Red Sea east coast of Egypt), with the Afroasiatic Egyptians, itself a formidable merchant-priest class-title system-clusters, likely sharing the merchant-priest class-title feature of highly valuing documents and the archiving of them, as was the case with the Phoenicians merchant-priest class-title, before the much later Moorish class-title influence overgrowing that of the original Phoenician, and the consequent takeover of Egypt.

Moorish-America Connection Lasting into the Early 19th Century

With the founding of the United States of America, the Moorish connection and conflicts with them could have been the remnants of the connection of the western last-cycled civilisation restoration centre with eastern North America (and rivalry within the class-title flexibility) in the collective mentality of the east coast indigenous American class-title system clusters that was, in turn, inherited by European settlers.

This would turn the rivalry into a north-south one within the broader western restoration centre itself as white European settlers mostly came from the European north, and Moorish system-cluster the Mediterranean. Therefore, in addition to being merely a coast-to-coast rivalry, it was a rivalry within the priest-merchant class-title system-clusters that stretched over the two restoration sub-centres, both the original and successor sub-centres, on opposite sides of the Atlantic shores.

Morocco, in 1777, was the first independent nation to publicly recognize the United States, in 1784 became the first Barbary power to seize an American vessel after the nation achieved independence. The Barbary threat led directly to the United States founding the United States Navy in March 1794. While the United States did secure peace treaties with the Barbary states, it was obliged to pay for protection from attack. The burden was substantial: from 1795, the annual amount paid to the Regency of Algiers amounted to 20% of United States federal government's annual expenditure.

This could be read as a Moorish effort to harass and deter white American settlers from moving into North America from the east coast where they have civilisational ties to and a more friendly rivalry with.

Card Kerrep Sewl I-21

Why were there two versions of the portrait of Napoleon, one fair-skinned and one dark-skinned?

Why was there a guild mentality along the historically German-dominated Baltic shores and the German-speaking regions?

Why did the House of the Blackheads in Riga under the Brotherhood of Blackheads, worship St. Maurice, the dark-skinned Moor?

Later Portrait-bleaching Campaigns of European Rulers / Aristocratic Class to Downplay the Moorish Importance in Europe

Alongside the northern restoration centre in Scandinavia, the Moorish as the southern restoration centre in the West had both genetic and cultural exchanges, partial assimilation and later ties with the former, and vice versa. Yet with the power of balance gradually tilting to the north's favour, document archiving was more and more 'processed' by them, with the use of bleaching to match their own fair skinned appearance.

This could also explain why some of the merchant-priest class-title system clusters throughout Europe had tanned skin as remnants of this Western survival branch in the south even after its peak of influence had long faded. Napoleon is the best example of portrait-bleaching campaigns where leading Europeans (French and the St. Petersburg-based German class-title groups plus west Slavic class-title group) did so to create an image of prestige linked to the European north in an effort to fight against 'Russia', which could have been the declining, yet still formidable force of Tartaria, having absorbed a noticeable west Slavic class-title groups into them.

The merchant guild / class-title system clusters in the Baltic regions worshipping St. Maurice, at House of the Blackheads in Riga, for example, is one such indicator of the Moorish presence in European history, with Brotherhood of Blackheads being the best indicator of this merchant class-title / guild mentality. This was passed down from early western restoration centre (with a bit of southern influence). With the medieval system of guild (notably the Hanseatic League) which Riga is part of, the apprenticeship is part of the legacy left by such class-title system clusters. Such remnants of the Moorish influence in the European restoration civilisations as far north as the northeastern corner of the Baltic shore, were the ones remaining under the radar, either because of Riga's relative periphery location, or its lesser influence in the cultural and political sphere.

Card Kerrep Sewl I-22

What did the Dutch discovery of Australia, Tasmania and New Zealand symbolise?

Why did the Dutch VOC allocate the same name — Zeelandia to New Zealand and the Island of Dutch Formosa?

Why was the name Staten Landt allocated to New Zealand, upon discovery, before it was changed to Nova Zeelandia?

What other factors other than economic ones contribute to the Dutch East Indies, or present-day Indonesia being crowned as the 'Netherlands' most precious jewel'?

Dutch VOC's Discovery of Antarctica through Australia, Tasmania and New Zealand and Their Deliberate Cover up: *Misallocating the Name Zeelandia to Formosa to Cover up the Fact that It Was the Same Name They Had Given to Antarctica*

First naming the fortress on Dutch Formosa Fort Orange in 1627, before renaming it Fort Zeelandia in 1628, and the later referring to the capital of the island of Formosa as 'Zeelandia' could have been to confuse the masses and distract them from learning about the true place they had allocated the name Zeelandia to, which was Antarctica. They discovered, through leapfrogging through Tasmania, what we now know as New Zealand after having discovered the former in 1624 (also the date that Dutch Formosa was established) and the latter in 1642 — a Dutch VOC's effort to spread disinformation.

Revoice - Uncurling The Involute Carrier of Reality

The many layers of confusion could perhaps be looked at from the perspective of how the official records of Fort Zeelandia, in Formosa suggests that it was changed from Fort Orange to Zeelandia, before the fortress changed names between the above-mentioned two for several times, with the same name of Fort Orange given to the one founded in New Amsterdam (present day New York) in 1624, again, the same year construction of Fort Zeelandia in Formosa started, creating a mental spatial-stretching and distraction.

Yet the later episodes of repetitive name changes of Fort Zeelandia in Formosa might have occurred only after the discovery of New Zealand, to scaffold up the confusion as the Dutch discovered such a place with its proximity to Antarctica, from which they possibly planned to recreate their earlier success in reaching Antarctica.

The name Staten Landt was allocated to present-day New Zealand by Abel Tasman upon discovery in 1642, before it was changed to Nova Zeelandia in 1645, serving as another layer of constant overlapping and re-allocating of the names of these places, particularly while the two names of Fort Orange and Fort Zeelandia were taking turns being the name of the fortress in southern Dutch Formosa.

Such complication of the already confusing mechanism was based on the forged sense of 'incomplete edition that needs re-editing', given the confidential and mysterious nature of the Dutch VOC, the way it operated through this name shuffling, to deter outsiders from trying to look into and grasp the advancement in geographical knowledge.

This could have been done deliberately as Abel Tasman, serving the Dutch VOC, was possibly using either older source European maps inherited from the last-cycle civilisation, or the Dutch VOC's discovery of those maps from 1603 onwards at Gunung Padung (meaning mountain of enlightenment) pyramid in West Java where documents are archived (either from Eastern restoration centres, Moorish-Phoenician / Viking-Vandalic western centre, or directly inherited from last cycle civilisation), and other such sites throughout Indonesia, as well as the newly-learnt folk lore description and know-how of sailing routes to Antarctica from the Māoris, who had themselves ventured there from New Zealand, to increase the success rate to regularise sailing to Antarctica

Card Kerrep Sewl I-23

What fuelled the Anglo-Dutch war other than rivalry and trade wars?

What did the British Empire inherited from the Dutch extensive monopoly in accessing and trading from Australia and New Zealand?

Potential Intentions behind Such Manoeuvre

Such manipulation was done so as not to go against their contemporary mentality current, which was a growing sense of civilisational superiority over all other ancestral civilisations, or to guard what they might had discovered in Antarctica, possibly an entrance to Agartha, that would have matched the surviving legend.

During the first three Anglo-Dutch wars (1652 - 1674) the Dutch intelligence was most likely infiltrated by the British, thereby causing the former's knowledge about and know-hows on regularising sailing to Antarctica to be revealed to the latter. The year that concluded the fourth and last Anglo-Dutch war in 1784 was just one year after James Matra's producing 'A Proposal for Establishing a Settlement in New South Wales'. This could be read as the intention of the British to sail south and take over the Dutch monopoly of accessing Agartha through Antarctica.

The rising power of the British Empire, especially with the technological breakthroughs could have been their selective learning of everything mechanic / materialistic from Agartha, while selectively dismissing any superhuman ability from the spiritual side (telekinesis, telepathy, dimension travelling) that could rival the mechanical side which would further solidify the materialistic view of such a version of science given how they had secured a dominant status in the narratives of human development at that point.

Card Kerrep Sewl I-24

Why did Nazi Germany take interest in Antarctica (beginning with Neuschwabenland) and Himalayan Bhö as it rose to a sea power that could challenge the British?

Tensions between Different World Super-powers or Rising Powers in regard to Accessing Antarctica Lasted Well into the Two World Wars

The later rise of Germany as a seafaring power that challenged the British monopoly, culminated in Nazi Germany's interest in Antarctica as well as Himalayan Bhö. Their breakthrough in submarine technology was a development based on the existing-concepts and models the British / Americans already had (they had acquired from Agartha with limited attempts of reverse-engineering), which they 'borrowed'. Later development well into before and during the two World Wars involved the Germans' 'further borrowing' from the British, French and the Dutch, before Hitler's expedition into Antarctica, possibly escorted by U-boats. The flying boat, equipped on the catapult ship, to photo Neuschwabenland was probably just the initial stage of accessing Agartha, which could have been accelerated by Nazi Germany's losing to the Allies and faking of its final downfall while leading some senior officers into Agartha, where they possibly perished.

Reference:

I. *Encyclopaedia Britannica* (EB) first edition had Terres Australis depicted where present-day Antarctica is located. Yet by the third edition, any terra near the south pole region was removed, showing just emptiness at the south pole on the map, before the modern 're-discovery' confirmed landing of Antarctica in 1895

II. *Thesaurus Geographicus* in 1695, from 'Countries about the Poles', shows what seems to be intentionally-crafted doubt about the shape of Australia while putting New Zealand and Hokkaido close to the North American West coast. This illusion of doubt could have been deliberately crafted or from confusion from reading the old source map inherited from the last civilisation, which depicted a much lower sea level during the last ice age, to deter interest in the new discoveries

Card Kerrep Sewl I-25

What preserved the remnants of Tartar system-clusters and vitalised them? How did contemporary Shadow Tartar states become what they are?

Epochs of Rivalry between the Priest-merchant Class-title System Clusters and the Tartar Counterpart, Shadow Tartaria, and Contemporary Stalemate.

The Pair of Kuahroom-Laong: dualistic, opposite, yet interconnected, self-perpetuating cycle from the Book of Changes; the True Identity of Russia and the Tungusic Jurchen-Manchu

The Tungusic Jurchen-Manchu were the Tartarian class-title system clusters who were mostly the herder / warrior-nomadic class-title system clusters that rebelled against and conquered the mainland East Asian leftover of merchant-priest class-title system clusters. Yet the Tungusic Jurchen-Manchu voluntarily merged with the features of East Asian merchant-priest class-title cultural features, the latter's population nearing 100 million in the mid 1660s, in exchange for the latter's obedience for the former to create effective rules as a minority in number.

From the perspective of the Tungusic Jurchen-Manchu, they might have lost their distinctive class-title features by late 18th century, yet the new hybrid creature that is mainland East Asian merchant-priest class-title now featuring Tartar features culturally and linguistically, as they've shed half of their own merchant-priest class-title features, tells a different story. This signals how the Tungusic Jurchen-Manchu class-title swept their Tartar cultural features into a shadow Tartaria state, instrumentalising the local priest-merchant class-title leftover features as camouflage, becoming a self-proclaimed priest-merchant class-title system clusters, all while keeping the Tartar class-title system clusters as an unchallenged dominant force for almost three hundred years until 1911.

This is the voluntary Laong (white) of the shadow Tartaria that is contemporary mainland East Asia where merchant-priest class-title features/values are held as the face, whereas with Tartar ones it was what is practised underneath the skin, first by the Tartar themselves, before the voluntary embracing of the Tartar features by the original merchant-priest class-title subject to the Tartar.

An originally non-Tartar class-title priest-merchant class-title, no more, happily running Tartar features — after the Tartars' voluntary merge with such priest-merchant class-title subject and their cultural leftovers still present back then — in contemporary times almost 400 years after.

On the other hand, the Himalayan Bhö by the point of the Tungusic Jurchen-Manchu Tartar expansion into and conquest of mainland East Asia, central south and Southeastern Siberia was already a shadow-Tartar state after the Tartar in the north, being fragmented and eliminated by the Slavic-Cossack class-title system clusters coalition, retreated into Himalayan Bhö.

Card Kerrep Sewl I-26

What is the contemporary shadow Tartar state aside from the one in mainland East Asia?

What was the Time of Troubles?

Why were there inconsistencies in different versions of the records of the Napoleonic War against 'Russia'?

What are the mental traits of Tartar class-title system-clusters and their shadow Tartar successors?

The Gradual Slavic Takeover of Siberian Tartaria and the Creation of Eastern Slavic Culture / Identity following the Conquest of Siberia.

Cossacks, a spin off Tartar warrior class-title system clusters, worked with the Slavic class-title groups that were expanding from Bohemia and Poland into the area of St. Petersburg and Novgorod area to rival and pressure the then Moscow-based western Tartaria by the mid 16th century. With the earlier form of the Moscow-based western Tartaria, the Golden Horde state led by the Mongol-Tartar, it can be seen as the Mongol-Tartar having forcibly made the western Slavic settlements as well as the para-eastern Slavic settlements that had settled the region before Slavic territories were expanded into Bohemia, which were still highly consistent and almost identical with their western counterparts at that point, assimilate into their Tartar class-title, thereby creating a demographically half-Slavic, half-Mongolic-Turkic Tartar-state.

Through the flexibility of the warrior-merchant-priest class-title system clusters, and their partial merging amongst one another, starting with Yermak Timofeyevich, the expedition campaign resulted in the complete conquest of Siberia, reaching the Pacific coast of Sea of Okhotsk by the late 17th century. With such a landmass and resources, the Slavic-Cossack class-title semi-merge were able to gradually out-manoeuvre and then encircle, assimilate the Moscow-based Western Tartaria into themselves, having cut it off from its eastern branches in Siberia that had been fragmented and assimilated into themselves. A corner that was involved in the western Slavic-Cossack class-title system-clusters merge, yet less under the spotlight would be the state later known as Ukraine.

It could be read as the natives having preserved their semi-nomadic, semi-Tartar, mobility-focussed mentality that could be translated into their tendency towards self-sufficiency and autonomy-seeking, while merging with the reversely migrating western Slavic merchant-priest class-title system clusters that settled there permanently.

This is quite distinct from the later Russian identity that was a northern route of the epoch of encircling the Tartar class-title system-clusters who gravitated towards a shadow Tartar class-title system-cluster given whom they merged with were Tartar class-title system-clusters instead of semi-Tartar ones.

The Time of Troubles in the late 16th and early 17th centuries in Russian history should be read symbolically as Moscow-based Western Tartaria in conflict with the eastward expanding west Slavic class-title system-clusters, who brought with them other Western European class-title system-clusters, such as the German and French-speaking ones that would later leave their marks on the famous city of St. Petersburg. By the time of the Napoleonic War, Western Tartaria was completely blocked from accessing the entirety of steppe-Tartaria, both because of the Slavic-Cossack as well as the Tungusic Jurchen-Manchu effort to shattering leftover Tartar powers there just half a century ago. Yet it's a complete opposite story on the Manchu side as it's a Tartar-led encroachment onto south eastern and southern central Siberian Tartar powers, mainly the Dzungar–Qing Wars between 1687 and 1758 that saw the Tartar Tungusic

Jurchen-Manchu-led Qing coming into conflicts with the Tartar-Mongolic Dzungaria where the former optimised the geographical resources within the landmass of mainland East Asian merchant-priest class-title territories they had previously conquered and eventually crushed the latter. The Tartar Tungusic Jurchen-Manchu were able to achieve this strategically through dragging down the Tartar-Mongolic Dzungaria enemy with their own disproportionally larger economy as well as technologically through the Jesuits' introducing of the more refined European-styled cannons, combined with their inherently specially-engineered half-pounder arrow-heads that could generate destructive powers greater than crossbows, rivalling even the musketeers, which was then topped up through forming a further duet with mounted archery, a Tartar tradition extremely flexible and untraceable in nature. After the conquest of Dzungaria, the Tartar Tungusic Jurchen-Manchu would complete its transition into a semi-Tartar class-title, or a shadow Tatar class-title. The Napoleonic War against 'Moscow-Russia' was the last fatal blow from a Slavic-Cossack and western European coalition to the remaining Tartar power west of the Ural Mountains, east of the Baltic states.

The Russian identity is the unconscious inheriting of Tartar cultural-class-title features, becoming a third-glaze standing on the high ground, looking at its former identity, European, and its former rival's identity, Tartar, which they both are, and aren't; noticing the in-between-space they've been in since.

While cooperating with the Cossack and absorbing the eastern side of Tartaria in central and Eastern Siberia during the epoch-stretching rivalry against the Tartars, the Slavic class-title groups immediately east of the Baltic have unintentionally inherited the war-like warrior features of the Tartar and to a lesser extent the Cossack class-title with the notable mentality applied to tactics being, one, salami-slicing / unnoticeable engulfment (passive-aggressiveness) on any of its rivals or obstacles standing between it and its goals.

Two, mastery of fear-creating, for example, an almost soul-piercing stare with complete silence and non-action as if the eye-contact moment between a lion and the prey, the only difference being the Tartar features would allow the predator to choose either to play a mental game and keep delaying that attack (passive-aggressiveness), or immediately doing so after the stare. The trick would be, to a lesser extent, to immediately initiate aggression, but it was more about prolonging that limbo-state of uncertainty and arbitrariness such 'plasticity' could bring to the target.

This is part of a forcibly-launched psychological battle, effectively minimising an opponents' mental reserve to make any move after the aggression is launched or rendering the opponents self-sabotaging as a self-perceived way to 'not trigger the monster (whose triggering lies in itself, not in the hands of the opponent)' both before and after the aggression is launched.

The last feature would be active-aggressiveness even at the cost of self-destruction, the 'I would rather see you lose than to win myself' mentality.

These features fit how the Soviet Union and the earlier Nazi Germany were run, with the latter's source of Tartar features possibly coming from Old Prussia, the place that was constantly interacting with and involved in any coalition initiated by either side (later including St. Petersburg) that passed down the Tartar features through their own gradual metamorphosis into a shadow-Tartar culture. Such features are still alive in contemporary Russia and parts of North-eastern Germany.

This is the non-voluntary Kuaroom (black) of the shadow Tartaria that is contemporary Russia where merchant-priest class features / values are held as the face, yet Tartar ones are what is practised. An originally non-Tartar class-title happily running Tartar features after the non-Tartar class-title's aggression and engulfment against Tartars, conquering the Tartar while absorbing their cultural features, extending them into something immortal with ghost features adorning the new hybrid creature.

Contemporary Geopolitics as a Quasi-stalemate between Priest-merchant Class-title System Clusters and the Tartar Counterpart

After millennia of pull-and-push struggles and rivalry, the priest-merchant class-title system clusters and the Tartar class-title system clusters, both of whom emerged after the collapse of last-cycle civilisation reached a quasi-stalemate.

Dead as Tartaria might have seemed in contemporary times, long after its apparent death by 1750 when the steppe Eurasia was closed. Its surviving North American branch started to be squeezed out of the landscape by 1850s (with European settlers absorbing mostly the priest-merchant class-title cultural features in North America), two shadow Tartar states, Russia and mainland East Asia together control Eurasia, who are only non-Tartar class-titles system clusters on paper and keep the Tartar essence perfectly alive in their borderline subliminal manner. They are on bad terms with and in a renewed rivalry against the contemporary priest-merchant class-title system clusters, the West, with the priest-religion part being replaced by materialistic corporatism or in essence, elitism-oligarchy-styled 'selective' capitalism. Yet, with contemporary corporatism having its roots in a Prussian-style educational system, where standardised labourers, rather than independent thinkers are trained, this in turn is a Tartar class-title cultural element. This cultural element slowly eclipsed the original capitalism that had its root in merchant-priest class-title systems, gradually having its operation transformed into those based on dehumanisation, in a passive-aggressive manner that was almost undetectable, dissolving targets from within, and utilising psychological coercion.

This can been seen as a sudden wake-up-call where multinational corporations, such as McDonald's, and world governments such as the Singaporean, the Pacific Polynesian and Melanesian, German, Canadian, British, American and Australian ones were concerned where they were revealed to be involved in behaviours gravitating towards shadow-Tartar system-clusters features.

Such phenomena, however, have been a long time in the making with the ease of re-spread and re-adoption based on lower-tier human mental structures used by Tartar system-clusters. Those blocking the true essence and consciousness in the sense of esotericism, gnosis, string theory in quantum physics, which are all cross-dimensional in nature, would be repetitively reignited and revived for the human species as long as the return to the last-cycle civilisation style spirituality and true mastery of essence, consciousness and DNA-digits was not achieved. That said, there was a brief period of Renaissance that experimented with the exploration of consciousness through psychedelic drug use in the 1960, albeit ending in drastic crack downs in the following decades.

Just as the notion of the 'End of History' was an illusion created by the perceived collapse, or declining of the shadow Tartar states back in the 1990s, the apparent death of Tartar features allowed them to survive as an undercurrent in history, which went on to parasitise the Western merchant-priest class-title system-clusters in the form of subliminally 're-ignited' Tartar features that were overlooked for relatively long periods of time, before multiple revelations of such parasitisation, predominantly with Russia, mainland East Asia, intra-independent organisations within the U.S. as well as Switzerland (instrumentalised as a base via its neutrality) involved, started to emerge as 'difficult-to-deny' phenomena in the mid to late 2010s.

Having made an in-depth comparison of merchant-priest and Tartar class-title system-clusters, one should note that Tartar is only Tartar by averaged frequency of these mental and cultural aspects taking place, as far as collective class-title system-clusters memories goes.

For instance, the Anglophone class-title system-clusters still have a hazy collective memory of their Anglo-Saxon and Celtic past, while holding an even hazier memory of the Scandinavians, the cousin their ancestors split from (around 2500 years ago), coming out of the Scandinavian peninsulas. This is why any contemporary Anglophone class-title system-cluster would have vivid image, or biases towards one another, slight image or biases towards the Scandinavians, and very weak, to non-existent image or biases towards other class-title system-clusters more remote to them. This is based on proximity to interactions, in addition to geographical or cultural similarity and dissimilarity.

This is why, with the Western Hunter-Gatherers refugees who themselves became aborigines of the Scandinavian mountain-island during Holocene epoch, or the Last Glacial Period global sea-level rise, as known as the great flood, along with the later migration waves of the Afontova Gora from the bank of lower Yenisei River Basin — where blond hair feature first emerged in Homo sapiens, with its descendant being the Afanasievo culture based around the same area, albeit expanded eastward towards the western shore of Lake Baikal, and the much later descendants being the city-states Kröran Kingdom, Kucha and the closely-related Saka-derived Kingdom of Khotan (the more powerful Sogdiana to the west was a close genetic and cultural relative) in the Tarim Basin, of which the Tocharians were the genetic and cultural cores — and the North Siberian ancestral to the Uralic class-title following a more northerly route from Arctic East Siberia, possibly joined by the a split of reverse Na-Dene migrations from North America back to northern Siberia where the other half contributed to the partial ancestral component of the Yeniseian class-title, the Anglophone class-title system clusters memory of them is non-existent as they had no mental interactions, let alone physical ones with them, or their descendants that are extremely difficult to locate.

The hazier such collective memory of other class-title system-clusters is, the weaker the image and biases of other class-title system-clusters a class-title system-cluster can hold or perceive.

This is why with the original refugees who settled the Scandinavian mountain-island as well as the aborigines there, the Anglophone class-title system-clusters' memory of it is non-existent as they have no mental interactions, let alone physical ones with them, or even their descendants that are extremely challenging to even locate.

Given how the extreme capacity of a collective class-title system-cluster could stretch back as far as 2500 years, it would be understandable that such image and biases towards the Tartar class-title group based on Mongoloid-looking populations lingers in contemporary times, excluding the Tartar remnant features and the more recent add-on factors of the history of the past century that have solidified Tartar features in some groups of Mongoloid-looking populations.

Such images and biases are average memories based on the frequency of the Mongoloid-looking populations taking on the Tartar, or shadow-Tartar class-titles, yet with the past exceeding the 2500 years mark, branches of Caucasian-looking populations were actually the dominant pillars of the newly-born Tartar class-title system-cluster then.

The reason that the above-mentioned biases are held by class-title system-cluster consisted of genetically Caucasian-looking populations is because throughout the past two thousand years, gradually, but subconsciously they have built up their image and biases towards class-title system-clusters made up of Mongoloid-looking populations based on interactions with them — a product of the Tartar class-title system-clusters, consisting of a genetically Mongoloid-looking population that rivalled the Caucasian-looking populations who were predominantly priest-merchant class-title system-clusters.

The transition from Caucasian-looking populations being dominant forces of the Tartar class-title to Mongoloid-looking populations was gradual, for the first emerging Scythian, Sarmatian and Saka Tartar class-title system-clusters were in fact genetically Caucasian-looking. However, this would slowly transfer to their successors, the Kuahong Nera, Teroong Gehera, Noonan and the later Huns and Turkic system-cluster groups, who, joined by the migration coming out of the Himalayan mountains and plateaus, became Eurasian-looking.

This trend was followed by the completion of the transition of Tartar class-title system-clusters into governance by Mongoloid-looking populations, by the time of the proto-Mongolic Khitan, Tungusic Jurchen, and later the Mongols and Manchus, around 1500 years ago.

Card Kerrep Lerats II
Erosion-reversing: Dialling into the Lost Faces of Mythologies and Religions

Card Kerrep Sewl II-1
What lies beyond the lava-filled crust and cores of the Earth?

Why is the Hollow Earth theory and Agartha a recurring topic of discussion throughout history?

What version of technology and science did the last-cycle civilisation hold?

The Landscape of Planet Earth beyond the Lava-filled Mantles and Core:

Touchable Physical Structures underneath Planet Earth and Respective Higher Dimensional Space bound to them, or 'Agartha' as an Umbrella Term Describing Such Higher-dimensional Spaces

The physical Earth, through geological studies, is structured as the following layers —

- Upper lithosphere, or continental crust (30 – 50 km)
- Lithosphere (40 km – 280 km) inhabited by Homo Subterraneous
- Asthenosphere (80 – 200 km, up to 700 km) inhabited by *Homo Subterraneous / lobster-headed*, or upper mantle
- The rest of the mantle are inhabited solely by *the lobster-headed* (700 km – 2900 km)

This is no-contradiction with the idea of hollow Earth, or Agartha, as Agartha is an umbrella phrase describing the higher-dimensional spaces that are bound with each of these physical layers of the Earth, using them as a cover in the three-dimensional domain, to retain its discretion under the trial-system accessible only to those who have mastered the spirituality, consciousness core and DNA-digits.

The reason why such lava and gravity-filled covers are still needed to maintain the trial system (which will be explored in **Card Kerrep Sewl V-1**) is because these Agartha tiers do not permanently exist in higher dimensions that deny access to any three-dimensional adventurer who desires to enter it, but instead constantly shift, vertically between higher (from the fifth-dimensional space onwards) and lower dimensions, the three-dimensional space, and horizontally between different parallel universes on the same level of a given dimension.

For example, shifting into a parallel world that is in the same three-dimensional space would create short windows where such access becomes temporarily possible if those adventurers come trained and prepared.

The reality is actually a spatial-time-dimension continuum, particularly deeper down in the planet where not-so-stable joints between different dimensions, horizontally, or vertically regularly collapse, causing the force behind the dimensional-shifting mentioned above. Agartha was understood by the last-cycle civilisation, part of who successfully ventured into that realm and settled there, yet the technical parts were lost generations down the restoration civilisation after the great flood, gradually turning it into an umbrella term that exists only in the mythological domain.

Card Kerrep Sewl II-2

Why have there been records of encounters with higher dimensions?

Why have there been humanoids with heads of lobsters, goats and ducks throughout world mythologies and in early religions?

What are the connections between world mythologies / religions and Agartha?

What does the Triskeles symbol symbolise?

Why is the construct of the Homo sapiens world full of man-made trials?

Breaking down of the Higher-dimensional, and Hidden Layers and their Corresponding Entities and Civilisations

In the shifting higher dimension space covered by lithosphere (40 km – 280 km) live the Homo Subterraneous, beings in the fifth dimension, who are successful adventurers from the last-cycle civilisation, accessing the uppermost layer of Agartha. Heading down one more tier into the asthenosphere, or upper mantle (80 – 200 km, up to 700 km), it is occupied by lobster-headed humanoids, beings in both the fifth and the sixth dimensions, with a Homo Subterraneous minority, while the rest of the mantle are dominated by the lobster-headed humanoids only (700 km – 2900 km). All of these higher-dimensional tiers are marked by an apricot orange light. The leftover records of their appearance on the three-dimensional surface of Earth are as the lobster-headed humanoids depicted as lobster-headed soldiers in mainland East Asian mythology, *Investiture of the Gods*, as well as Japanese mythology.

Going deeper to the outer core (2900 km – 5100 km) camouflage, it is marked by a mint-green light and is inhabited by the alternate-goat-headed humanoids, beings in both the sixth and the seventh dimension, with their special gnarled roots / wooden body as manifestations in the three-dimensional world that constantly goes all the way up to the uppermost asthenosphere, sometimes even into the lithosphere.

They had a friendly relationship with the Homo Subterraneous up there, yet the three-dimensional branch of their manifestation was constantly hunted down by the last-cycle civilisation adventurers from the surface when they ventured down. Such behaviours from Homo sapien adventurers are a result of how the three-dimensional manifestation of the alternate-goat-headed humanoids spread, what the surface humans called 'wooden disease' very effectively.

This triangular relationship would ultimately result in the permanent de-coupling of the Homo Subterraneous from their Homo sapien cousins, on the surface. The leftover records of the goat-headed's appearance on the three-dimensional surface of Earth are common in Highland Scottish folklore, while Khnemu is known as an Egyptian mythological deity, Daksha in Hinduism and the wooden-bodied goat as a partial manifestation on the surface in mainland East Asian records of supernatural events - *In Search of the Supernatural*.

Revoice - Uncurling The Involute Carrier of Reality

At the deepest layer of the Earth lies a shifting-higher dimension covered by inner core (5100 km – 6378 km), which is marked by a purple-indigo light, blue grass, floating islands and trees using rapid growth to move at the speed of light (different species from the roots in the alternate-goat-headed domain). This shifting-higher dimension is inhabited by the duck-headed humanoids, beings in both the seventh and the eighth dimension, who are the creators of Homo sapiens and the main judge of the trial system where three-dimensional beings are tested on the surface, before they could advance into Agartha.

Most Homo sapiens failed the trial and some tried to cheat the system and venture into the Agartha realm, only to be faced with complete body and partial consciousness core dissemination. The Homo Subterraneous is one big exception among early Homo sapiens who marginally passed the trial and successfully ascended into the Agartha realm. Such structure of the Earth's reality could also be part of the source influence of why Homo sapiens are naturally tilted towards designing systems with trials, which are often self-involving and supported by other sub-trials.

Though present at every tier in Agartha, as well as on Earth's surface, the wooden element that coexists with the duck-headed humanoids in their realms is the size of a tiny floating island, in the shape of a human leg and consists of an infinite number of parallel arms bound with and overlapping one another.

Two reflections on the Earth's surface of such entities could be found in the Triskeles symbol, featured on the flag of Isle of Man, which has its origin in symbols from Sicily, which in turn have a Moorish class-title origin connecting to Agartha and to the duck-headed realm, or Bodhisattva's Thousand Arms, a symbol of the infinite number of higher-dimensional wooden entities that glow a grey, clay-like fluorescence, that portrays the structure of such arm-cluster floating leg illustrations in the duck-headed realm at a sub-quantum level well beyond nanotechnology.

The leftover records of the duck-headed appearance on the three-dimensional surface of Earth are as god of the sun Ra, Horus, Monthu, Seker, and Thoth as Egyptian deities in the Egyptian mythology system, god of the sun Garuda in Hinduism, Kuwaharmtero (beak-headed) in East Asian mythology *Classic of Mountains and Seas*, while the Korean Inmyeonjo, Slavic Gamayun are reverse versions of it, with Homo sapiens heads and bird-based bodies, a result of a partial duck-headed manifestation through possession of Homo sapiens.

Additionally, Gwaihir the giant eagle in J. R. R. Tolkien's Middle Earth could be seen as a corrupted depiction of the duck-headed, with the accurate depiction of their location in the 'Middle of the Earth'. In a similar sense with the non-possession approach of manifestation done by goat-headed humanoids, as they do through gnarled roots and trees, any non-humanoid form of supernatural creature featuring an avian head could be a partial manifestation of the duck-headed in the three-dimensional world. The 'god of the sun' symbol found in many mythologies could be read as the three-dimensional cover at the inner core of the Earth where the duck-headed humanoids are located, with the high-pressure, condensed lava and beam resembling the sun.

They are also seen as death (and continuation into the afterlife or passing the trial to access Agartha for those who are trained enough) in addition to power and sun in Norse mythology as Hræsvelgr, or Corpse Swallower, in its Hel (hell).

Card Kerrep Sewl II-3

How does the extra-terrestrial entity relate to those within planet Earth?
What was the outlook of Homo Subterraneous?
Where did the dinosaurs go?
How is the coyote entity related to the dinosaurs?

Higher Dimension beyond Inner Earth's Cover, the Coyote Domain

Beyond the higher dimensions, shifting underneath the multiple layers of Earth under the three-dimensional cover of lava and high pressure, there exist dimensional-shifts that would allow even higher dimensions, under cover of the broader universe, or other universes, to link to the Earth's core.

Despite holding the highest level of intelligence and mastery of its own consciousness and DNA, the duck-headed humanoids had to become apprentices of entities with even higher mastery of all these, who are able to shift between even more dimensions vertically and parallel universes, horizontally. Such masters are the coyote entities, beings in the eighth dimension and several dimensions up.

While the duck-headed humanoids are prestigious enough to walk the pitch-black mountain, dimensional-shifting consisted of dimension-continuum, coated with pink fog and transparent grasses, before reaching the partial manifestation of the coyote as a giant spiralling head in that realm, the goat-headed humanoids and Homo Subterraneous are not lucky enough to qualify to be pupils there. The goat-headed and Homo Subterraneous did not get to the place themselves as the duck-headed humanoids had, but were 'transferred' into that realm by the coyote entities with protections provided as that realm would otherwise be too high of a dimension for them to endure. With the dimensional membrane protection provided, they had to function as part of the coyote realm, as part of their pre-trial-climbing course trial, by half-dissolving themselves to shift into that space. The result of this is that the coyote realm, in addition to the black mountains, pink fog and the transparent grasses, is also filled with hill-size goats and the elongated skulls of Homo Subterraneous, with their sizes not much smaller than the goats, curling like overly thickened chameleon tails. Despite this being a manifestation and despite the disproportionate size of the skull, this is an accurate depiction of the appearance of Homo Subterraneous, with elongated skulls that curl as if they were chameleon tails, which is recorded in the so-called lizard-humanoid encounters by Homo sapiens, not to be confused with dinosaurs. The latter had ascended into a realm that is of even higher dimension than the coyote realm, with their base a starting point no lower than the fifteenth dimension. The remnants of their remote influence on Earth could only partially be seen in their cousin, the duck-headed humanoids and the chameleon-tail-like skull of Homo Subterraneous, possibly because of preoccupation with other works in their higher dimensions.

Just like the ascended dinosaur-humanoids, the exact three-dimensional, or even fifth-dimensional cover the coyote used to manifest fully in the lower realms is not known yet, with the range of possibilities ranging from dimensional shifts between the fifth and seventh dimensions to our galaxy or parallel universes of our universe. In this sense, though, the coyote, their avatar in the three-dimensional world, the dog-headed humanoids and the dinosaur-humanoids originally from Earth, could be regarded as truthful aliens, a hyper-Earth type, non-native to planet Earth.

Card Kerrep Sewl II-4

Why was cynocephaly a widespread phenomenon throughout world mythologies and folklore?

What is the relationship between the Japanese mythological Yokai (monster) Tengu and the coyote entities?

Why do Tengu wear wooden clogs?

What motivated civilisations around the world to make and wear Kahrokka, the one-piece robe, religiously?

What is the role of Homo Subterraneous in Earth's trial system?

The Coyote Entity's Partial Manifestation on Earth

The coyote entities and their dog-headed subspecies have their partial manifestation on the three-dimensional Earth's surface as recorded in cynocephaly by the Egyptian gods of Set, Hapi and Anubis, the Dog People Land and the dog-headed mounted raiders in mainland East Asia (Classic of Mountains and Seas & In Search of the Supernatural), the dog-headed people Indici in India, Mahakh the dog spirit in Aleutian culture, Poko Kachina the dog spirit in Hopi (Arizona) culture, Saint Christopher in medieval Europe, with were-hyena and werewolves being a relatively more incomplete partial manifestation of them through possession of humans.

The master-apprentice relationship between the coyote entities and the duck-headed humanoids are probably the best recorded in the Japanese Tengu (meaning sky dog) who is a supernatural entity combing avian eagle-wings and coyote-dog-like facial features with a beak-like nose and wooden clogs on the feet, portrayed as an evil spirit who possess humans, leaving their subjects in amnesia and disorientation if, indeed, the human targets survived.

The hidden message that should be seen symbolically is the wooden clogs on the feet of the Tengus as they could be seen as an animated wooden shoes, having their own sentience and awareness. To understand such an animation process, the Wooden Disease needs to be explored briefly. It is campaign the Homo Subterraneous helped launch on the arrogant and ignorant type of Homo sapiens on the Earth's surface, with the permission and with help from the duck-headed humanoids, while the main executioners are the avatar manifestation of the dog-headed, with the tree roots stretching into the layers of Earth that is the domain of Homo Subterraneous and that stretches all way up to the surface of the Earth, being the catalyst for the Woodenising symptoms known as the Wooden Disease (the whole process will be explored in **Card Kerrep Lerats IV**) among the Homo sapiens. This is best recorded in the Black Death styled plague, in Homo sapien history, again needing to be read symbolically.

It is through those gnarled roots of the trees known as the Gnarled Platform that animated wooden items such as the wooden clogs the Tengus are wearing come to be. Their role in the launch of Wooden Disease is one of monitor and reporter (while creating drug-like effects on Homo sapiens) where information about Homo sapiens' arrogance, negligence and the negativities stemming from them are shared with the main executioners, the dog-headed humanoids.

The essential part of the onset of the symptoms is the visual effect created by the dog-headed humanoids through swinging the overly wide and loose sleeves of a one-piece robe, known as Kahrokka. Once eye-contact is established with the targeted Homo sapien individuals, the microorganism symbiosis in the Homo sapiens bodies would start to destabilise, with the worse effect being the automatic shutting down / locking of more DNA, leading to the final physical malfunctioning through sometimes a gradual, but more often a rapid woodenising of the body.

As long as there's no arrogance or negligence in selected groups of Homo sapiens, they could choose, and many did, to become the co-operators of the Kahrokka-wearing dog-headed, as they put on their Kahrokka and subliminally swing the sleeves to create the desired effect. Yet these groups of Homo sapiens didn't have the capacity to launch the infection through creating the visual effects, if they did not approach the dog-headed avatar to 're-supply' the supernatural ability granted to them.

Throughout time, even the non-co-operator humans put on the Kahrokka one-piece as a symbol of guardianship and good luck and to protect themselves from the Wooden Disease. This can be seen in the one-piece robe design of ancient costumes throughout the Tartar class-title, Scythians; the priest-merchant proto-Tocharian class-title (who broke away from the pre-Tartar proto-Scythian and proto-Saka class-titles, their genetic cousins also having descended from the Afanasievo culture where fair skin and blond hair are also inherent, yet not blue eyes), along with multiple other class-titles system-clusters within the priest-merchant class-title system-clusters continuum, such as Ainu, Jomon, mainland East Asians, Tlingit, Alaskan Taku (its name translates into the Geese Flood Upriver Tribe, which could be depiction of the duck-headed realm) in North America, to the class-titles in the Andean Ranges of South America. Integrating the Kahrokka, the one-piece robe, into the costumes was perhaps the one issue the Tartar class-title and the priest-merchant class-titles both agreed on. However, such defensive use of Kahrokka by the priest-merchant class-title originally had a more active use when the knowledge of and access to herbal mixtures were present — the swinging of the Kahrokka sleeves when used with psychedelic herbs helped them better access the higher-dimension as part of the practise of passing the trial. Yet the knowledge was lost down the generations and Kahrokka became a signal of peace and a plea to be spared by the dog-headed humanoids.

Another Homo sapien attempt to honour and thank the dog-headed humanoids for sparing them from the Wooden Disease is the subliminal use of the word Kotka (meaning eagle, which could be seen as an variant of the duck-headed) in Finnish. This very name was given to a town in Southeastern Finland, not long after Finland escaped the Black Death relatively unscathed. The word is phonetically referring to Kahrokka, the one-piece robe worn by the dog-headed humanoids and its Homo sapien co-operators, carrying the meaning of 'eagle' only as a reference to the duck-headed humanoids who permit the coyote entities and their dog-headed avatars to do so, minimising the mention of the latter so as to avoid irritation.

Card Kerrep Sewl II-5

What is dimensional-shifting and its connection with the 'Absolute'?

Why were records of astronomical anomalies common throughout history?

Why were records of encounters of 'worm holes' common throughout history?

Why are mechanisms of creation such as DNA sequence constructed in a self-involving manner?

How does the self-involving mechanism translate into one's perceived three-dimensional world?

Constant Plasticity in the Inner Core of Earth, or the Duck-headed Tier of Agartha

The duck-headed land is a place where the 'absolute' is present. It's a no-space-chaos phenomenon where there are endless possibilities through the 'plasticity' as nothing has come into form. Such no-space-chaos coexist with the duck-headed humanoids. This is recorded in Eastern esotericism as 'ancestors of ten thousand things' that are the embodiment of abyss, emptiness and nothingness.

The duck-headed is one such entities who master both the involvement and the detachment of the process of 'absolute' manifesting into 'forms', who in turn learn the craft from the coyotes, to the point that they are in control of the dimensional shifting process where floating, space-tearing dodecahedrons spiral into more complicated dimensional-shifting structures such as icosahedron and hepteract, creating even more spaces throughout different dimensions in the process. Such self-involving mechanisms could also be observed in many of the creation laws regarding the three-dimensional physical world, such as the DNA sequence, the way events unfold in a broader picture, or trial-like systems designed by three-dimensional beings, as being compatible with the self-involving mechanism. This renders plasticity; while being incompatible with the essence of such mechanism, on the other hand, renders chaos, disturbances and destructions, themselves a balancing power in the duality of the three-dimensional world.

Think of a flattened-out highway systems with no possibility of going the other way to return, or without any design of circles, that ramps and exits rely on for changes of travel directions. Such a flattened highway system is the embodiment of incompatibility with the self-involving mechanism, which brings chaos. The highway systems we are familiar with would be a great example of being compatible with the self-involving mechanism, creating dynamics, possibilities of movements, mobility and changes.

Yet such a poorly-designed highway needs to exist somewhere in one's perceived world so as to serve a driving force (counterbalance to

To name a few:

Rauravam (torment of snakes) / Mahararuravam (death by snakes)

Both of these should be read as adventurers; being devoured by the serpent entities guarding Agartha, sentient, non-humanoid entities in Agartha. These entities are also reported during psychedelic 'trips', which are themselves temporary access to the higher dimensions, loosely connected to Agartha.

Kumbhipakam (cooked in oil)

This should be read as being cooked by the lava, the three-dimensional cover of Agartha inside Earth.

Sukaramukham (Crushed and tormented)

This should be read as being crushed by the gravity and pressure as the three-dimensional cover of Agartha inside Earth.

Andhakupam (Attack of the animals)

This should be read as the attacks from either the manifestation of the lobster-headed, goat-headed, or duck-headed in Agartha as warning signs to the adventurers who violate the trial system.

Sarameyasanam (Torment from dogs)

This should be read as attacks from the coyote avatars as the dog-headed in Agartha.

Avici (turned into dust)

For the more trained adventurers who ventured close to the duck-headed land, they could have been crushed by the 'absolute-manifesting-into-form' process, having been crushed by the cross-dimensional shift of the space.

Ayahpanam (Drinking of burning substances)

This should be read as the Homo sapien's digestive system being filled by the lava, the three-dimensional cover of Agartha inside Earth.

Paryavartanakam (torture from birds)

This should be read as the attacks from the manifestation of the duck-headed.

Card Kerrep Lerats III
Unsolved mysteries: Midland between Coincidences and the Pre-determined

Card Kerrep Sewl III-1
Why are certain geographical locations prone to choices of spiritual practise and supernatural sightings?

What are the origins of the flying head entities recorded throughout East, Southeast Asian and South American folklores?

Three-dimensional Reality as Spatial-time Continuum, Horizontally (parallel universe) and Vertically, Leading to Occasional Encounter with 'Spatial-shifting'

A few geographical features on the surface of the world are said to be spiritual, reflected in many traditions, as a result of their proximity to joints of the spatial-time continuum, thereby the proximity to fluctuating spatial-time cusps, increasing the chance of encountering the 'dimensional-shifting' in the three-dimensional realm of the Earth's surface. This dimensional-shifting is usually in the shape of highly complex, recursive, involving balls, radiating beams, or the 'cracks' created in the sky that could be mistaken for the Aurora Borealis.

These features are fluvial terraces, mountain tops and the deep-sea realm with the deep sea being a realm that could connect with the lobster-humanoid, sentient whales. Whale worshipping is the remnants of 'dimensional shifting' events symbolised throughout the coastal Homo sapien cultures.

Following the symbolic reading of 28 different kinds of hells in Garuda Purana being failed attempts to access Agartha, disregarding the trial system set up by the duck-headed, not all adventurers are trial system violators. Some may have actually passed the trial, unlocking their consciousness and

DNA, and gained the right to dive-ascend into Agartha but ventured too far and were then faced with dimensional-shifting that was beyond their ability to handle. The result is the partial dissolution of the consciousness and total dissolution of their physical bodies, distorting them into in-between-space creatures that are neither Agartha or Homo sapien.

Records of such in-between-space creatures could be found as flying, floating, disembodied head entities throughout Southeast Asia, mainland East Asia, the Japanese archipelago, the Andean region of Chile and Argentina. They appear as Nukekubi in Japanese, Krasue in Thai, Leyak in Indonesian, Penanggalan in Malay, Kirrerakmtero (fallen head) in mainland East Asia and Chonchon in the Andean region. This is the result of the aforementioned partial dissolution of their consciousness and total dissolution of their bodies as a result of their overconfidence, in turn a product of the rich knowledge they inherited from the last-cycle civilisation, likely the Mu continent branch, about accessing Agartha. This could have led them, after passing the trial, to attempt access too far down the tier, into Agartha.

Another possible scenario that made the floating head entities what they are were rushed attempts to access Agartha, instead of looking for highland islands, or frozen near-pole coasts when the great flood hit, without properly passing the trial on the surface, resulting in their bodies being cut off and their consciousness being largely shattered while doing so, even in the shallow tiers of Agartha.

Card Kerrep Sewl III-2
What role do the flying head entities play in Earth's trial system?

One of the Three Contributors to the Wooden Disease aside from Kahrokka-wearing Dog-headed Humanoid and Homo Subterraneous

The floating head entities hold the ability to generate extremely high frequency air vibration, which could occasionally destabilise the spatial-time continuum joints and open up dimensional-shifting openings. They are triggered to generate such high frequency sound waves when hit by any sort of beam, or shooting-based weapons, as opposed to the Homo

Subterraneous, their cousin that ascended into the higher-dimensional underground earlier, who animate wooden artefacts and send them back to the surface to create the same sound waves effect, a catalyst to inflicting the Wooden Disease on Homo sapiens.

The floating head entities, like many other beyond three-dimensional ones, would be taken as evil if perceived only on a superficial level.

Similar to the Japanese Tengu, a combination of the dog-headed avatar and the duck-headed one, the existence of the floating head entities, without their own noticing, contributes to the equilibrating mechanism the duck-headed humanoids help strengthened through inflicting the Wooden Disease on the Homo sapiens with arrogance, negligence and any accumulating negativities stemming from these two natures.

Card Kerrep Sewl III-3

What lies beyond the symbolic stories in Finnish mythology and East Asian folklore?

How does esotericism apply to the three-dimensional, physical world?

Other Hidden Existence in Eastern Folklore and Esotericism

In Eastern esotericism, there is the concept that translates as:

'For, in him, a buffalo would find no butt for his horns, a tiger nothing to lay his claws upon, and a weapon of war no place to admit its point. How is this? Because there is no room for Death in him.'

One possible reading of this is the Homo sapiens features in the esoteric texts had passed the trial, mastered basic level of dimension-shifting, including the altering / shifting of the spaces around himself / herself and him / her body itself into a higher dimensions, creating a spatial-time continuum, or fluctuating cusps, thereby rendering any pure three-dimensional physical assault ineffective on his / her body.

Another case is secret deals made between the above-mentioned Homo sapiens and the floating head entities, with the former temporarily borrowing the body and space-shifting power left on latter, therefore achieving such non-touchable state.

Such deals could also be struck between sentient animals such as the whales, brown bears and the flying head entities, while parallel deals with the same effects are struck between the dog-headed humanoid avatar and their coyote core.

In Finnish mythology, Kullerva summons up bears and wolves from the woods and has them appear to be harmless cows while herding them towards Ilmarinen's wife. When the herds of harmless cows are close enough to the target, Ilmarinen's wife, he had them turned back to bears and wolves to kill her. A dog-headed humanoid was actually involved and turned itself into a rhinoceros to be among the cows, moving with them towards Ilmarinen's wife. Then it used the dimension-shifting ability borrowed from the floating head entities reversely, to shatter the body of the target into pure digits, all while remaining untouchable, making any resistance against it, impossible.

The dog-headed avatars don't necessarily have dimensional-shifting powers as they either have to communicate with the duck-headed humanoids, or their coyote core to have access to such ability. Striking a deal with the floating head entities would be a much faster way as they are disoriented and easy to 're-direct', as opposed to the strict 'filtering system' dictated by the duck-headed and their coyote core they would otherwise have to go through.

An even more dramatic use of such borrowed power from the floating head entities is recorded in the mainland East Asian folklore, where a general named Lereeon Geirterar had inflaming blades attached to the oxen horns and torches bound to their tails, before directing them to charge into the enemy's invading army that had previously almost annihilated the state (the state was in essence vast territories united and governed by originally duke-like local kings with the fiefdoms originally being the source of such territories, before the local kings' decentralising from the 'central king', rendering themselves perceived central kings that fought with one another for hegemony) the general served, kick-starting the beginning of the turning of the tide of war.

A sentient brown bear, gaining its sentience through Homo Subterraneous' 'Kirerool' animating tunnel and Gnarled Platform shape-shifted itself into a bison and charged shoulder by shoulder among the other oxen, while also passing the 'dimensional-shifting' ability it gained from the floating head entities to other oxen's horns. This utilised the ability, reversely, in the same manner as in Finnish mythology — weaponising the dimension-tearing power to dissolve the enemies' bodies into digits, while staying untouchable themselves, through the entire process.

Yet, when the general's troops were cleaning the battlefield that consisted entirely of the enemy troops' corpses (as they expected given there were zero casualties on the side of the general who organised the flaming oxen charge), only circular slice-shaped torsos corresponding to where the soldiers' belts were found, with all the belts remaining unscathed. The non-touchable nature of the belts stemming from the dimensional-shifting ability, in this case, is demonstrated through how they had protected the circular, salami-like slices of the bodies.

The general, suspected that whoever had manufactured the belts must have mastered esotericism and he was partially correct. Without the knowledge of the sentient bear disguised as a bison who borrowed the dimensional-shifting ability from the floating head entities, such abilities could be equally achieved by Homo sapiens who passed the trial.

The abilities used in both the oxen and the belts are from the leftover powers from previous Homo sapiens, although in the case of the non-touchable belt, the deal might have been struck by other sentient animals remaining hidden in the dark other than, or in addition to the brown bear, with whom possessed the basic dimensional-shifting abilities (mastering esotericism) and who, upon over-diving into deeper tiers of Agartha were distorted into the in-between-space being that are the Kirrerakmtero, or Nukekubi, and many variant names describing the same entity.

Card Kerrep Lerats V

The Bloated Detachment of the Supernatural from Us: Codes within Us that Link to the Ground of Reality

Card Kerrep Sewl V-1

What is the structure of reality made of?

How is a duck-headed led trial passed?

What potentials lie in the locked parts of Homo sapien DNA?

What is the structure of the different layers of human bodies?

How are ancient mega structures related to the mastery of DNA and consciousness?

Why have superhuman abilities been recorded in history?

Consciousness, its Relationship with Encrypted DNA-digits and Superhuman Ability after Unlocking them

Having explored the structural ground of the physical reality as spatial-time-dimensional continuum, the units that they consist of are now to be explored — digits. Digits as in being made of information-digits.

The physical bodies of Homo sapiens for example are created upon the information-digits stored in DNA sequences. For Homo sapiens and its ancient, ascended predecessors to pass the trial, they had to tap into the true core of their consciousness, lying from the fifth to the seventh dimension, connected through a digit-based cross-dimensional digit-thread to their physical brains, or the three-dimensional branch of consciousness. This is well-recorded in Himalayan Bhö, Hindu and Western gnosis traditions where the physical body is coated by the etheric / vital body (between 3D and 4D realm), the astral / emotional body (between 4D and 5D realm), the mental body (between 5D and 6D realm), the causal body (between 6D and 7D realm) and the essence / consciousness (in the 7-dimensional realm), which could become connectable and thereby accessible through further understanding and mastery of esotericism and spirituality, through the practise of meditation, use of psychedelic herbs, tunes and tempos and dances that generate certain waves of frequency. Once the individual's essence returns and becomes adept in connecting with the consciousness core in the higher dimensions, the digits stored in the DNA start to be unlocked.

The Digimon anime series in contemporary time has had the concept of a digital world (Internet-based) materialising into a physical one, while forcing a merge with the human physical world. This could actually be read as a symbol of how the human three-dimensional world is itself consisted of information-digits, even before the creation of Internet within it. The merge depicted, in the series, in this sense, is a symbolic indication of how the world is finally being forced to come to the realisation of the real ground of reality — its building blocks being digits and how higher dimensions are products of digit-based dimensions, recursing into expansions that ultimately far exceeds the micro-scale of nanotechnology, thereby crossing the dimensional thresholds into something non-perceivable for three-dimensional sensory systems, or even those of the higher dimensions depending on the gap between the tiers of the dimensions.

The Homo sapiens from the last-cycle civilisation had deep understanding of this, and therefore quite a noticeable number of them accessed Agartha and established the Homo Subterraneous realm before the great flood. Having gradually unlocked the parts of DNA not designed for the immediate three-dimensional world survival mode, they gained telepathic, telekinetic abilities and shape-shifting ability on physical items outside of their own bodies. The stage of the shape-shifting ability could be seen as a fringe land, transitory into the next, final dimensional-shifting one. The shape-shifting performed on a physical item, fuelled by the DNA digits and radiated through the physical human brains could be both a physical alteration, namely, the dissecting of the targeted particles at near quantum level, moving them to a designated space, before reconstructing the particles back into their pre-dissection structural configurations that consist of the item as well as a vertically upward manifestation-projection into the higher dimension where the physical item targeted had been successfully transported there, crossing the dimension borders. Such physical items could then be partially transported back to the three-dimensional space, partially fulfilling the concept of 'It is there, at the same time it is not there; it is here, at the same time it is not here.'

An example of a practise performed on a horse, saw a horse with its body consisting of cooked salmon slices adjacent to one another, leaving plenty of empty space where magnetic fields and lightning are holding the slices together, so they could float alongside one another, forming the horse's body. This partially represents the horse body having been shape-shifted as well as a partial projection of it, first to the fifth-dimensional realm and then partially back to the three-dimensional space, with the choice of cooked salmon slices being the elements that were nearby, in both dimensions, and the closest essence to the performer; all accomplished by the digits of the human DNA. Note that such semi-dimensional-crossing ability, at this stage, could only be performed on physical items, excluding the human perfumers' own body.

Finally, the dimensional-shifting ability, or self-teleportation dimensional self-teleportation would be reached. First to the performer's own body within two spots of the three-dimensional Earth surface, then horizontally to parallel three-dimensional universes, and finally vertically into higher dimensions. Time, from the point of Homo sapiens' vertically self-shifting into the higher dimension(s) on, would be perceived by them as cyclical instead of irreversibly linear as is the case for other Homo sapiens, bound only to the three-dimensional world.

Before the final stage is reached, there's no accessing Agartha and if forced attempts are made before the final mastery stage of consciousness and DNA digits on dimensional-shifting, they would be faced with hell-like consequences, as mentioned previously — being shattered into pure digit units by the dimensional-shifting force in Agartha.

What those trial candidates did before reaching the final stage was well-recorded in the knowledge they passed down to restoration centres after the great flood — one of which was using the super-human ability to build mega architectures that mechanic-based devices could not achieve. The Egyptian pyramids are one of the many examples, possibly through the coordination of multiple superhuman abilities such as teleportation, shape-shifting, telekinesis, and telepathy.

Card Kerrep Sewl V-2

Why have locations with enclosed natures been chosen for long-term meditation throughout history?

The Undead, yet Hibernating Potential in Homo Sapiens

Enclosed spaces and physical isolation are recorded to be either mentally and physically devastating, causing claustrophobia, or ascending where the Homo sapiens individual / individuals emerged at a completely different level, with an ascended spirituality. This is because for those who have the talent to pass the trial while not being too absorbed into and solely bounded with the three-dimensional cangue, they would be given a tremendous push-forward in such enclosed spaces to conduct mind-consciousness exploration, laying the foundational work for the later unlocking of DNA digits, if they ever proceeded to that level.

Card Kerrep Sewl V-3

What are the mental effects of changes in physical human body structure?

How are sound and sound waves related to the physical human body structure?

Why were there records of extreme mental status change where blizzard, gales and in some cases mountain tops were the physical surroundings?

Why were ancient languages stubbornly guarded against linguistic and phonetic corruption?

External Factors that Could Alter the Digit Configurations in Human Brain and Bodies

In addition to the previously mentioned Wooden Disease where high frequency sound waves and gnarled roots altered human DNA digits, further worsening the Woodenising symptom, another less-extreme example was the rise of Tartars as global class-title system clusters and powerhouses.

Starting as semi-warrior class-title system clusters from the last-cycle civilisation, the turning point of the proto-Tartar class-title that really separated them from the priest-merchant class-title system clusters via their metamorphosis into distinction was their geographical surroundings — extreme-rigidity-bringing anticyclones and the snow-gale-fuelled air vibration that altered the digits in their brains, or even body structures in a cymatics sense, given that seventy percent of the physical human body structure is made of water, or the three-dimensional physical branch of their consciousness, with the brain being the centre of it.

The relevance of sound wave frequencies, their vibration in the physical human body structure, through resonation, or a more invasive change of human physical body structure, and in turn the mental status and cross-dimensional bodies, reflects on the common usage of spells, vocally read-out, or sung-out words, which are sound waves themselves, in last-cycle civilisation and its restoration civilisations. One good example is the positive mental status change due to an upward advancement through the cross-dimensional bodies through which the ancient Sanskrit mantra system would catalyse, which partially derived from the Shintasha culture, a descendant culture of Yamnaya, likely with substantial portion of the cymatics technology inherited from the Kumari Kandam refugees. Similar phenomena were also observed in the spiritual practises through vocal spells in other Indo-European languages, proto-Himalayan Bhö, proto-Austronesian, proto-Kra–Dai proto-Hmong–Mien language, proto-Ainuric, proto-Inuit, proto-Na-Dene languages and so on, mostly occurring through strong inheritance of spiritual aspect of cultures from the last-cycle civilisation, among the priest-merchant class-title system-clusters.

Such physical body structure-altering effects of sound wave vibrations would be the contributing factor to the Tartars' potential intermittent, unstable communications with the wild horses (up until the former's complete domestication of the latter), their superhuman strength and skill in mounted archery, synchronisation with their horse mounts, their mastery of both their passive-aggressiveness and active-aggressiveness and the salami-slicing shadow, unnoticeable, cooking-frog-in-warm-water-style, engulfment of their targets, the more powerful the targets, the more so. However, given the non-severity of the digit alteration, in comparison with Wooden Disease, the Tartar class-title system clusters that were re-absorbed into the priest-merchant class-title system clusters would see such features gradually declining, if not completely fading away.

Card Kerrep Lerats IV

Fears towards the Shattering of our Body Structure: What Is the Truth behind Diseases?

Card Kerrep Sewl IV-1

How are Homo sapiens connected with Homo Subterraneous?

How do the subterranean tree roots relate to diseases?

How are the wooden artefacts 'animated'?

Where do microorganisms, in symbiosis with human physical bodies, come from?

How do high-frequency sound waves relate to the Wooden Disease?

How is Wooden Disease triggered?

The Origin of Wooden Disease and Tunnel beyond Mechanism to the Subterranean Realm

There exists a Kirerool tunnel system, or tunnel of the mechanism behind, between the Homo Subterraneous realm and the Homo sapiens surface, with a single-way access upward from the Homo Subterraneous side. The latter cannot even conceptualise such ideas, let alone be aware of its existence.

A hermit-type of Homo sapien, who dwelled mostly in dense forest, however, knew this. They were the groups having passed the duck-headed based trial, before themselves ascending into Homo Subterraneous. Using their immunity against the high frequency sound waves (as they have partial access to the dimensional-shifting skills, rendering themselves unaffected), the hermit-type actively acted as a balancing force as they deactivated all the animated wooden artefacts, such as rice scoopers, pillows, animated by the enormous, gnarled root system that stretches all the way up to the surface forest, sent up by the Homo Subterraneous.

The exact role of these wooden artefacts in launching the Wooden Disease is how they could generate high frequency sound waves that could alter the physical structure within the bodies of Homo sapiens, particularly the microorganism-symbiosis, the brains, and their DNA in a cymatic sense. This would open up windows for the microorganism on trees to overtake the ones already in Homo sapien bodies, leading to body malfunctioning, along with the shutting-down of the Homo sapiens' DNA, caused by the high frequency waves. Such effect could be further optimised from the sound waves resonating with the particles on the ground where Homo sapiens settled.

This is made even more complicated as the microorganism originally came from a comet and had dominated the surface. Trees could also animate wooden artefact yet chose not to re-animate the animated wooden artefact sent up by Homo Subterraneous once deactivated by the hermit-type. They would instead choose to animate the corpses of Homo sapiens once their bodies were completely Woodened, had ceased functioning and were rendered corpses.

Neither Homo Subterraneous, nor the tree-microorganisms were worried about the spread of Wooden Disease slowing because of the hermit-type's counterbalancing, as both parties were aware of the animated coin units sent by the former, which could attach themselves to the hermit-type in hibernating mode, before self-activating in secret and flying to Homo sapien settlements to generate high frequency sound waves.

From the perspective of the tree microorganism, a third-party player, just like the hermit-type, the Wooden Disease is referred to as Project Slender Waist — as in rendering the waists of the Homo sapien minds and thinking capacity slender for the few Homo sapien survivors.

All in all, these are all relatively catalysing, auxiliary measures as the core finishing trigger of launching the Wooden Disease lies in the visual effects created by the hyperactive Kahrokka-wearing dog-headed humanoids and their Homo sapien cooperatives, swinging their Kahrokka sleeves.

The balancing role of the hermit-type semi-Homo sapiens at the cusp of ascending into Homo Subterraneous is also the reason why after the last wave of them accessing Agartha, there remained no one with a true understanding of the Wooden Disease, allowing the disease to wipe out an astronomical number of the Homo sapien population.

Card Kerrep Sewl IV-2

What are the perceived causes of Wooden Disease?

What are measures taken by Homo sapiens to solve the Wooden Disease problem?

What role do the goat-headed humanoids play in Wooden Disease?

Perception of Wooden Disease among Non-co-operator Homo Sapiens (unaware of the true nature of it)

The permanent symptom, in additional to the fatal Woodenising symptom, for Homo sapien survivors, or those whose Woodenising did not spread as fast across the bodies, is the 'Eye Open' Symptom where uncontrollable eye openness blocks blinking ability. However, despite any knowledge regarding the Kahrokka-swinging dog-headed humanoids,

Homo Subterraneous' animating power on wooden artefacts, coins, the Kirerool tunnel connecting their realm and the Homo sapiens', the tree microorganisms, and even the hermit-type that helped mitigate the spread a bit, the Homo sapiens perceived the Wooden Disease and the Eye Open Symptom as the result of consumption from self-meat-filling cooking cauldrons and referred to the disease as Filsel.

The Homo sapiens took three major measures they thought would help them recover from Filsel; wearing the Eye Armour, testing themselves using the Gerleraon Ongwaeras, also known as Sugar Anachronism testing toolkit to see if they're infected, and creating underground cave-houses surrounded by gnarled roots to slow the spread of the Woodenising symptoms. Yet, unbeknown to them, two of the three measures actually accelerated the spread of the disease and worsen the symptoms, creating even more deaths (which would come back to haunt them and spread the Woodenising symptoms even further once the Woodenised corpses were re-animated by the tree-microorganisms).

The Eye Armours are armours that require holes drilled into the skulls, chick bones, and shaving of hair for the device to fit. Supposedly creating protection from eye openness, they are actually designed by the dog-headed humanoids to block parts of the visual effects as they do not wish to see their subjects die all at once, but rather want to enjoy the process without it being realised that they were behind it.

The Sugar Anachronism testing toolkit was created by the less-wise among the hermit-type who chose to re-join the Homo sapiens at their settlements. The use of it was popularised by the Homo sapiens through their own mass hysteria, fears regarding the fatality and the speed at which the disease was spreading. Yet the system is soon corrupted, first by manipulation of parameters of such testing, followed by the creation of asymptotic patients, labelling the healthy, non-infected as patients, justifying the actions to deprive them of mobility and autonomy, followed up by the financially tempting side for the statisticians in charge of the testing to falsify the reports to create on-and-off report results so that more patients had to return for the testing, or be deprived of mobility, allowing them to fulfil their desire to enjoy policing the subjects, to enhance their personal wealth through extra financial rewards, to contribute to the further solidifying of a narrative they're integrated into, or to protect those close to them who are weaponised as potential hostage in a blackmail.

The gnarled roots caves the patients are put in are actually part of the Gnarled Platform, the extension of the forests in the Homo Subterraneous realm that are capable of percolating through Homo sapien patients and that tapped into their shut-down DNA (from the visual effect and the high frequency sound waves), causing them to lose limbs, other organs, large, deep portions of the bodies (that dissolved), as opposed to the surface of the bodies Woodenised by just the visual effects and the catalysing of it, before having wooden replicas refill those losses. This was all while extracting DNA and brain matters having been force-uploaded there to the Gnarled Platform (as digits). That is why the patients usually came back from the underground caves even more Woodenised, or dead, with those surviving having half of their intelligence, consciousness as well as half of their original body portion and organs taken away, therefore the tree-microorganisms' referring to it as Project Slender Waist of Homo sapien minds.

Aside from the counter-balancing nature of Wooden Disease launching jointly executed by the dog-headed humanoids and the Homo Subterraneous against the manifestation of negligence and arrogance among Homo sapiens, the goat-headed would take some of the selected Woodenised Homo sapiens from the Gnarled Platform, where their own manifestations are as wooden goats, back to the Agartha tier of the goat-headed humanoid, as a second chance given to the Homo sapiens who had fallen into arrogance, negligence and related negativities, although they originally had a high potential of passing the trial.

The Woodenised Homo sapien corpses would be re-purified and appear as sentient platypuses later sent by the goat-headed to be hiding with the wooden goats in the Gnarled Platform as avatars standing by, should there be any equilibrating actions needed in the three-dimensional surface.

Card Kerrep Sewl IV-3

Why were there records of 'moving wooden artefacts' throughout history?

How is Edgar Allan Poe's story *A Cask of Amontillado* related to the moving wooden artefacts?

Records of Animated Wooden Artefacts in Homo Sapiens History

Wooden flying birds as well as automatic wooden oxen were recorded as mechanic-robotic inventions in mainland East Asia, while Saqqara Bird were recorded in Egypt, both as restoration centres from the last-cycle civilisation.

Instead of pure mechanism, the creator, in this case, esotericism practitioners, could be the ones having encountered Homo Subterraneous during the latter's mission to the surface (as the knowledge of how to re-activate the Kirerool tunnel were lost to Homo sapiens, making them passive) and learnt the true nature of the gnarled roots of thousand-year old trees, discovered the Gnarled Platform and what it is capable of, and most of all, learnt the craft of animating wooden artefacts from the Homo Subterraneous manifestation on the surface and had those wooden birds and oxen animated.

Another possible scenario is that they had achieved a consciousness status close to passing the trial, re-discovered the know-hows of activating the Kirerool tunnel, or the tunnel beyond mechanism, and were favoured by Homo Subterraneous as candidates to access their tier of Agartha, tasked with bringing animated wooden artefacts to the surface as part of the balancing act.

Another such record could be found in Edgar Allan Poe's *A Cask of Amontillado* where the raven mask Montresor wore was the one who had cast the material onto the tiers where Fortunato was trapped, transforming him into a talking fork later, all unbeknown to Montresor, who believed the genius murdering of Fortunato to be his own masterpiece. The raven mask was a self-disassembled part from an animated wooden raven artefact.

Card Kerrep Lerats II

Erosion-reversing: Dialling into the Lost Faces of Mythologies and Religions

Card Kerrep Sewl II-7

How is unlocking DNA and consciousness related to the construction of ancient mega structures?

What did the ancient mega structures symbolise?

How did religions look like pre-last-cycle civilisation collapse?

What were the distortions / corruptions of the original last-cycle civilisation religions?

What did the sun-worshipping through mega structures symbolise?

What were the functions of the ancient mega structures?

Project Restoration and the True Form of the Mega Towers throughout World Mythologies (to reach God, a symbol of attempting to reach the same level of spirituality the predecessor last-cycle civilisation held)

High-rise Towers and Megaliths on Elevated Regions

At the initial stage of the Project Restoration where refugees from the three centres of the last-cycle civilisation, Kumari Kandam, Mu and Atlantis retreated to mountain-based islands, Arctic shores and plateaus, the knowledge and mastery to spirituality, consciousness core in the higher dimension, as well as DNA digits remained relatively unscathed. Using their superhuman ability, this was a prolific period for these restoration centres to build megaliths, pyramids and high-rise towers as both a reminder to keep reaching the same level of spirituality to pass the trial and access Agartha as well as energy, electro-magnetic field, celestial body, cosmos-energy (all digits they were aware of) drawing configurations.

Yet, upon losing hold to those masteries and knowledge, these structures became the corrupted version of reminders as well as instruments for the restoration centres Homo sapiens to use in attempts first to reach 'gods' again, a symbol of attempting to reach the same level of spirituality their predecessors had held, before further evolving to 'hopefully reaching gods' and total amnesiac towards such notion that was wrapped up with formality-based, institutionalised and complex ritual systems.

Religions, starting from this point also corrupted from some knowledge of Agartha and passing the trial to access it, to remedies and alleviators to somehow loosely keep the emerging egos and voices in the minds from not exploding at an irreversible level of destruction as untamed desires released by the blocking and loss of the accessibility to the digit-thread, which binds the cross-dimensional structure of a three-dimensional branch of the human brain to its consciousness core in the higher dimensions. This would result in the violence and cruelties inflicted upon fellow Homo sapiens, where the corrupted version of religions managed to stop complete self-elimination and extinction of the Homo sapiens species. Of course, there was only so much a limited-use version of religions could achieve, resulting in all the chaos in Homo sapien history after the retreat of the last-cycle civilisation and its gradual degeneration into oblivion.

Both the original last-cycle civilisation religions and the later corrupted versions of them can be found recorded throughout world mythologies as sun gods, symbolising the duck-headed humanoids at the core of Earth / Agartha, linking back to the very purpose of constructing these structures — to reach these 'sun gods'.

The so-called extra-terrestrials recorded as having manifested on the three-dimensional Earth surface are the creation of the even higher-dimensions-occupying coyote entities. Therefore, if any of the sun-gods were borrowed versions by the Homo sapiens from their interaction with the extra-terrestrial manifestation in the three-dimensional Earth surface, then the 'sun gods' in this context could be seen as referring to the coyote, instead of the duck-headed entities.

The best example of such a structure, built to reach the sun god is the Babel tower (Babilim in Akkadian), a high-rise tower (Etemenanki ziggurat) built in ancient Mesopotamia to reach the sun god of Utu in the Mesopotamian Gilgamesh mythology (the Hurrian equivalent of the solar god Shimige).

The global merchant-priest class-title system clusters, in this regard, held on to the heritage of the original religions for much longer than the forming and rising to power of Tartars as the rigidity and anticyclones of Tartar lands both altered their brains, body structures as well as singling out the need of survival, which would, in turn, have pushed them faster into a shift into heavy focus on the materialistic side / view of the world. Shamanism among the Tartar could be a re-spreading of such religions from the merchant-priest class region back into Tartaria, or remnants, a corrupted version of what they inherited from the last-cycle civilisation, depending on the varying rate of degeneration within their own class-titles, sub-versions and sub-divisions of them.

Another significant function and contributor to the slower degeneration of the original religions in the merchant-priest regions was first, the straightforward function of the structures being shelters for the refugees of the last-cycle civilisations, then the vertical agriculture that was operative in those structures. The vertical agriculture was vital in cultivating hallucinogenic herbs as aids of accessing the consciousness core in the higher dimensions and the unlocking of DNA digits in addition to staple grains. Remnants of such practise can still be found in present day West Africa in Cameroon and South America in Amazonian Peru and Brazil.

Card Kerrep Sewl II-8

Who were the guardians against the distortion / corruption of the original last-cycle civilisation religions?

How were the naming of the Jew class-title system-clusters related to Agartha and the last-cycle civilisation religions?

What role did Zoroastrianism play in such distortion of corruption of the original last-cycle civilisation religions?

Distribution of the High-rises, Megaliths and Records in Mythology

Distribution of such structures could be found across the globe in instances such as Gobekli, Tepe in Turkey, Ggantija Temples in Maltese islands, Machu Picchu in Peru, the Egyptian pyramids, Baalbek in Lebanon (Hajjar al-Hibla in Arabic), Gunung Padung pyramid in Indonesia, megaliths in Southern Siberia (before the rise of Tartar class-title) and the more recent Quinta da Regaleria in Portugal, serving their respective gods in the many corresponding mythologies.

Quinta da Regaleria would stand out among those ancient structures not just because of it being a more recent construction, but the Gothic-Vandal class-title system clusters (western restoration centre, north) and Moorish class-title (western restoration centre, south) who ruled over it. The so-called Knight Templar were another collective class-title name given to all the Jewish class-title, namely a class-title who resisted the gradual corruption of the original religions and fought against the 'progressive view' of post-Jesus Christianity that further derailed from the Agartha, higher dimensional realms knowledge through systemic disinformation and deliberate omissions of already encrypted messages within the Bible.

Three symbolic word units were used to refer to them: Jew-related variants, Stein-related variants and light-related variants. 'Jew' and its variants have been names referring to the originating place (which stretched from the westernmost point of the western restoration centre south, Morocco, Mali, all the way to Anatolia, the Eastern Mediterranean coast, particularly Judah) of such class-title in the Hebrew Bible, before the name spread to the eastern restoration centre, such as the Teews and Aleutian through the still present seafaring technology used by last-cycle civilisation migrants, post-great flood.

Stein means stone (the mainland East Asian Staon class-title was one such eastern restoration centre influenced, or that received refugees from the same class-title in Atlantis), referring to their knowledge regarding what is underneath the Earth, which are lava-filled stones as three-dimensional camouflage for higher-dimensional realms consisted of and existing among dimension-shifting, or Agartha, whereas the Licht (light in German), Litz (lightning in German) referred to their knowledge regarding either the duck-headed realm of the Earth's inner core as sun, or the intelligent, truthfully extra-terrestrials who are partial manifestations, or avatars of the coyote entities horizontally from the stars and vertically from beyond the 7th dimension.

Zoroastrianism, as another earlier universal religion post-last-cycle civilisation collapse, integrated the idea of 'sun god' as 'light' into its main belief system in a much more straightforward way and resisted the corruption of the original religion it inherited longer, after its initial corruption (from the original religion to symbolic-reaching of god), before further descending from henotheism to monotheism, and from profound spiritual connections with those higher-dimensional 'gods', to the formality of gods and much later a god.

⌐· ☽

Card Kerrep Sewl II-9

Who were the dark sages during the times of distortion / corruption of the original last-cycle civilisation religions?

How did humans start to be dominated solely by emotions, desires and inner voices?

How did this episodic corruption of religion relate to the Tartar class-title system-clusters?

Monopoly of Original Religion Remnants and the Rise of the Dark Sages

In the twilight epochs of the mastery, knowledge of consciousness core and DNA-digits as well as the growing unstable accessibility to, or the 'presence' of Agartha among restoration centres, the 'dark sages' inevitably emerged, their teachings immediate consequences of the gradual loss to the knowledge, thereby the misinterpretation and practises that were passed down through their teachings. These might have included the teachings of the need for human sacrifices through being bitten to death by snakes so as to be connected with Agartha guardians with the similar reptilian cymatic digit-shape, a corrupted understanding of Agartha guardians' true role both involuntarily and voluntarily, or striking a deal with the truthfully extra-terrestrial microorganisms brought to Earth by the comet to Homo sapiens, locking the Homo sapiens into a permanent biological symbiosis and reliance on the microorganisms.

This acted as a catalyst of the already emerging egos / desires among Homo sapien minds after losing hold of consciousness / spirituality and Agartha teachings, further contributing to the negativities those Homo sapiens created and the acceleration of the original corrupting of the religion to fit the new mental needs of Homo sapiens bound heavily and solely with the three-dimensional aspect among the worlds Homo sapiens consciousness extend to (its core lying in the 7th dimension), with actions driven by materialistic conditions and egoistic mental forces.

Such a catalysing role of the dark sages would further intensify the brain-body-altering effects from the rigidity and gale-snow-fuelled high-frequency sound waves in the high-latitude inland restoration centres, that resulted in the final rise of Tartaria and Tartar as a collective class-title system clusters.

Card Kerrep Lerats III
Unsolved mysteries: Midland between Coincidences and the Pre-determined

Card Kerrep Sewl III-4
Why were records of spirit possessions from animals widespread among world mythologies and folklores?

How are the sentient animals related to the Homo Subterraneous and Agartha?

How is Edgar Allan Poe's story *The Black Cat* related to the sentient animals?

Spirit Possessions and the Sentient Animals as Executioners

Black Cat, the Irish Elk and their Relatives

Recorded throughout Native American traditions; Western traditions as well as central, eastern, southern African; East, Southeastern and South Asian traditions, the concepts of spirit possession are usually collectively organised into religions such as Shamanism, Judaism, Christianity, Vodou, Buddhism, Hinduism and Shintoism, which in essence are all descendants, or variants of the last-cycle civilisation beliefs.

The animals that are believed to be responsible for launching the spirit possession are held sacred and viewed in awe; perceived as either being possessed by higher dimensional entities, or themselves being higher dimensional entities manifesting in the three-dimensional world. While they are both the case, what is being missed is the animals gaining sentience through their own potential of qualifying for having passed, or nearing the passing of the duck-headed trial just as the Homo Subterraneous did it, or doing so through the ability to absorb the animating force from the Kirerool tunnel and the Gnarled Platform connected to the Homo Subterraneous realm, which are monitored by the Homo Subterraneous.

These non-humanoid form sentient animals would work and settle in the fifth dimensional realm with the Homo Subterraneous once they pass the trial. They are the guides, guardians to Agartha, and regulators of dimensional-shifting, or the transportation, camouflaging side to Agartha that were recorded by later Homo sapien adventurers.

One such case recorded is hidden in plain sight in Edgar Allan Poe's *The Black Cat* where the protagonist attempted to kill the second black cat only to have killed his wife — a deliberate scratching that is perceptionally superficial and act of encrypting of what happened. In actuality, the protagonist's wife had already been possessed by the sentient black cat who qualified for having passed the duck-headed-based trial and manifested into the black cat from the shell, which was the wife, indicating that the second black cat had already possessed the wife and dwelled inside her brain and DNA-digits, before the encounter with the protagonist.

The protagonist's violence and easily irritable nature that led him to kill the first black cat Pluto (which was also a sentient cat, faking its apparent death) was the result of him being possessed by an Irish elk, or Megalosaurus giganteus, a sentient animal both qualified for having passed the duck-headed-based trial as well as having absorbed the 'animating force'.

The wife's body later became a rare contributing route towards the flying head entities (Kirrerakmtero, Nukekubi, multiple variants of names referring to the same entity) as it was re-designed by the possessing black cat to be excluding of the body below the neck. The dimensional-shifting ability in this case would stem from the parasitising sentient black cat, instead of the flying head.

The flying head with the dangling neck was later seen flying around the fjords in Greenland, one of the many merchant-priest class-title restoration centres culturally and spiritually, closer to accessing Agartha, with the black cat occasionally being seen standing on the cliff of the fjords when manifesting. When it did so, it would be wearing the minimised shell head and neck on its own neck as if a scarf.

In regard to the major reason why the Irish elk became extinct, it was simply that the complete species passed the trial and accessed Agartha, and that unlike the black cats who still have three-dimensional branches of presence, the limits of using the animating force from the Gnarled Platform for auxiliary purpose of dimensional ascending within the duck-headed trial system is that no lower dimension presences are allowed upon ascension, leaving their various deer cousins behind in the three-dimensional Earth surface.

Card Kerrep Sewl III-5
What are the roles of the sentient animals?

Role of the Sentient Non-humanoid Animals on Earth's Surface
The role of these sentient animals, viewed structurally in the duck-headed-led system, is to create a balancing mini-filtering system within the balancing system of Wooden Disease launching itself where the sentient animals select individual Homo sapiens, fallen to negligence, arrogance and the related negativities, to pass their 'possession mini-trial' just like the goat-headed manifestation in the Gnarled Platform, before a second-chance is given to those individuals to later access Agartha with these sentient non-humanoid animals. The only difference between the two is that there's a higher chance of Homo sapien individuals with talent passing the trial to be spotted on the Earth's surface by the sentient animals, as opposed to a more episodic surge in chance when Homo sapiens collectively hide in underground roots-surrounded caves. They hide for fear of dying from the Wooden Disease, and therefore are spotted by the goat-headed manifestation there, otherwise, when the disease isn't spreading, it would be rare for the goat-headed manifestation to spot such individuals.

The deeply-asleep consciousness of these selected Homo sapien individuals are teleported to the higher-dimension for a second-chance of refreshing themselves, with the result of the refreshing being the key to whether they pass the mini-filtering system held by the sentient non-humanoid animals.

That said, another role of theirs on Earth's surface is to help catalyse the launching of the Wooden Disease as these sentient animals are all too capable of generating high-frequency sound waves.